KNITTING SOCKS FOR BEGINNERS

Quick and Easy Way to Master Sock Knitting in 3 Days

By Emma Brown

Copyright© 2015 by Emma Brown - All rights reserved. Printed in the United States of America.

Copyright: No part of this publication may be reproduced without written permission from the author, except by a reviewer who may quote brief passages or reproduce illustrations in a review with appropriate credits; nor may any part of this book be reproduced, stored in a retrieval system, or transmitted in any form or by any means – electronic, mechanical, photocopying, recording, or other - without prior written permission of the copyright holder.

The trademarks are used without any consent, and the publication of the trademark is without permission or backing by the trademark owner. All trademarks and brands within this book are for clarifying purposes only and are owned by the owners themselves.

First Printing, 2015 - Printed in the United States of America

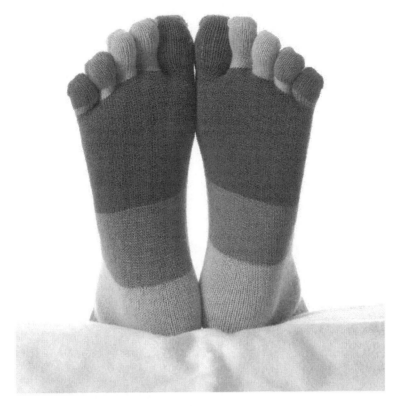

"You choose your friends by their character and your socks by their color"

TABLE OF CONTENTS

Introduction	1
The Right Tools and Materials	5
Choosing Yarn – All You Need to Know	9
Yarn for Socks – What's Available	14
Selecting the Right Knitting Needle	18
2 Ways to Hold Needles and Yarn	24
Understanding Patterns	27
Knitting Charts	29
Start Knitting	33
Finishing Your Project	55
Stitches	59
Knitting Techniques	83
The Double Point and Circular Needle Methods	115
The Double Pointed Needles	115
Means of Avoiding the Ladder Effect	120
The Stay Loose Method	121
Sock Sizing	125

Constructing Socks	127
The Cuff	128
The Heel	133
The Instep	142
The Foot	144
The Toe	147
Sock Patterns	155
Top/Down – A Basic Sock Pattern	157
Absinthe Socks	163
Tube Socks	169
Toe-Up Socks	175
Plain Socks	181
Blasted Toe Socks	191
Air Raid Socks	205
Fair Isle Socks	211
Tips for Long Lasting Socks	219
Top 5 Tips for Beginners	221
Left Handed Knitting	223
Top 3 Common Knitting Mistakes	225
FAQ	235
Conclusion	243
Knitting Glossary Terms	245

About the Author 251

INTRODUCTION

Being able to knit socks by hand is a **highly desirable skill that will change your life once you have mastered it yourself!** At least 40% of the worlds socks are made in China, but wouldn't it be better if you didn't have to rely on standard patterns, and the exactly the same footwear as everyone else? Wouldn't it be better if you could knit them for yourself – or even as gifts for your friends and family?

This book covers everything from the *very basics of knitting*, to *beautiful patterns* that once you have gotten to grips with, you'll be able to tackle any other knitting project easily. You won't be able to find a more comprehensive guide, that will take you through everything step-by-step, giving clear instructions and pictures to assist you.

This book is ***designed for beginners*** – people who have no experience with knitting whatsoever, ***but it can be used by anyone***. If you have a working knowledge of the basics of hand knitting, you will simply be able to progress to the patterns quicker!

For the beginner, socks can be very intimidating as knitting projects go, but you will soon realize how attainable sock knitting really is. The only prerequisite to socks knitting is in **knowing how to cast on, knit**, as well as **purl**. This guide will of course demonstrate very clearly how to complete all of these stitches, plus a few more to help you.

Now you may know that the history of knitting is vague – no one is entirely sure when it started and many countries stake claim to inventing it, but it may surprise you to learn that the very early knitting was actually confined to making socks and women's stockings – so as you can see, creating socks by hand has been around for an extremely long time!

Knitting is a skill that is commonly associated with being relaxing, but I bet you didn't know that it also holds a lot of health benefits too. A 2012 study conducted by the *Mayo Clinic* found that the hobby is therapeutic, can lower blood pressure and can uplift your mood, making you feel much more positive. So as hobbies go, the benefits of this one just keep coming!

Even though there are numerous creative pursuits out there, **knitting by hand allows one to knit reasonably well with little effort.** All you need is perseverance. There may be several other hobbies that derive satisfaction, even then, knitting leaves you with something tangible that you made from almost nothing; something warm, comfortable and that which you can use day in day out.

Here are a few ***facts and statistics about knitting*** that have been compiled by the *Craft Yarn Council of America* that may interest you:

Where people knit:

- Northeast 22%
- Southeast 24%
- Midwest 28%
- West 11%

- Northwest 7%
- Southwest 8%

Age range:

- 15% were 18–34 years old
- 13% were 35–44
- 23% were 45–54
- 32% were 55–64
- 17% were 65+

Why they knit?

- Feeling of accomplishment (93%)
- Reduced Stress (85%)
- Improved Mood (68%)
- Sense of confidence (56%)

Internet usage:

- Finding patterns (90%)
- Getting new project ideas (67%)
- Purchasing yarn, patterns and supplies (42%)

Print resources:

- Knit and crochet magazines (64%)
- Books (61%)
- Free tear-off patterns (59%)

- Projects on yarn labels (47%)

These stats simply show the wide range of the people in America who do knit, and it certainly isn't just older people! It's a hobby that is ever increasing in popularity, and once you have tackled all of the tasks this book presents for you, you will be able to see why.

THE RIGHT TOOLS AND MATERIALS

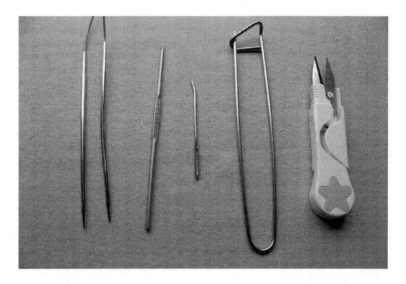

So now that you have decided to get to grips with hand knitting, and in particular sock knitting, it's time to look into the necessary equipment you'll need to get started. When you are a beginner, it's tempting to get one of everything, but that is so unnecessary! If you do, you'll end up with a lot of items you won't ever use. That being said, there are some things you do need.

For you to be able to knit socks, you will require *knitting needles* that are appropriately sized, some good quality *yarn*, very *basic knitting skills* and of course the *passion for the project*. It is also advisable to get a *knitting bag* that is well equipped which will enhance the pleasure in knitting and the success of your endeavor.

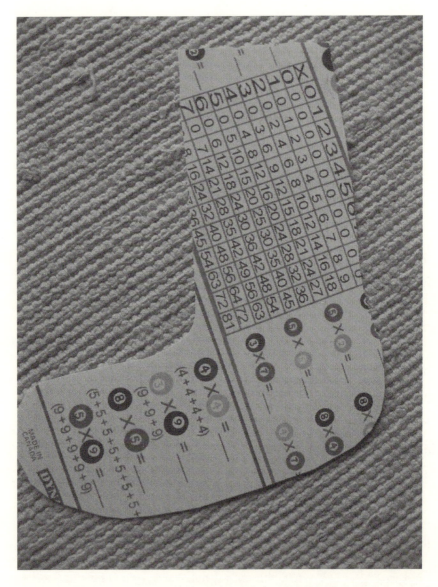

I would strongly advise that you go to your local haberdashery store, and pick up:

- Double point needles or even one or two circulars of reasonable size

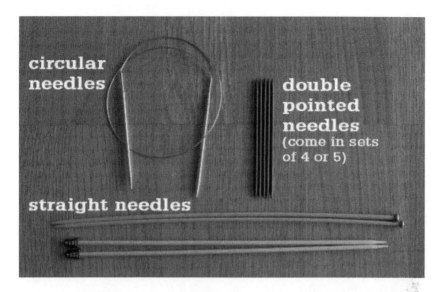

- Enough yarn for the exercise since every pattern requires an exact amount of yarn. If you don't have a specific pattern in mind to begin with, just get a range of colors and weights so that you have a selection to practice with.

- The stitch and needle gauge that contains an inbuilt ruler together with holes for measuring the size of the needle

- A measuring tape that is retractable, which shows both inches and centimeters

- A large eyed sharp needle and blunt tapestry needle

- Coiless safety pins and plastic stitch markers

- Yarn sniper or a small pair of sewing scissors

- Crochet hooks in a variety of sizes; the hook should be a bit smaller than the needles that you are using to avoid stretching the stitches when in use

- One small eraser and pencil

- Note pads that self-stick

- A fully functional knitting bag

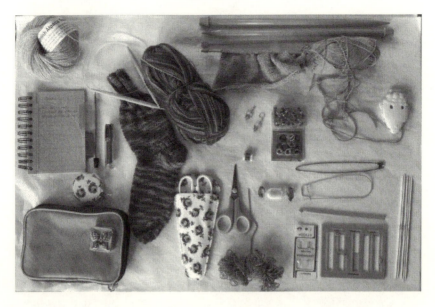

There will always be someone on hand in a shop that sells knitting equipment to assist you with getting hold of the items on this list.

The following items may also be useful in addition to the following requirements:

- Point protectors of knitting needles if not the double point needle holders that will enable stitches not to slip from the needle when not in use

- If you intend to modify the sizes of patterns, a small hand calculator will come in handy

- The toe and sock heel reinforcement thread or yarn.

Choosing Yarn – All You Need To Know

In the olden days, it was an easy task to select sock yarn. The weight yarns that were available mostly came in baby colors. More often than not, they were available in acrylic. This is a contrast to what we have locally available today in the yarn shops. Now you are able to get your hands on a wide range of colors, textures, weights and on top of that, there are many websites that allow you to purchase yarn from the comfort of your living room.

There are three main types of yarn; **wool, cotton** and **acrylic**. Each type produces an entirely different result after it has been worked with, so it is important to familiarize yourself with these during the practice stages of learning this skill so you know how each one works and how they suit you and your knitting style.

When **choosing a yarn type for your knitting project**, consider the following:

- **Wool:** Wool (made from the fleece of sheep) is the queen of yarns, and it remains a popular choice for knitters. Here are some of your wool yarn options:

    - *Lamb's wool*: Comes from a young lamb's first shearing.

    - *Merino wool*: Considered the finest of the fine breeds.

    - *Pure new wool/virgin wool*: Wool that's made directly from animal fleece and not recycled from existing wool garments.

    - *Shetland wool*: Made from the small and hardy native sheep of Scotland's Shetland Islands.

    - *Icelandic wool*: A rustic, soft yarn.

    - *Washable wool*: Treated chemically or electronically to destroy the outer fuzzy layer of fibers.

- **Fleece:** Examples include mohair and cashmere, which come from Angora and Kashmir goats, respectively. Angora comes from the hair of Angora rabbits.

- **Silk, cotton, linen, and rayon:** The slippery, smooth, and often shiny yarns.

- **Synthetic:** Including nylon, acrylic, and polyester. Straddling the border between natural and synthetic are soy, bamboo, corn, and other unusual yarns made by using plant-based materials.

- **Novelty:** Novelty yarns are easy to recognize because their appearance is so different from traditional yarns:

  - *Ribbon*: A knitted ribbon in rayon or a rayon blend.

  - *Bouclé*: This highly bumpy, textured yarn is composed of loops.

  - *Chenille*: Although tricky to knit with, this yarn has an attractive appearance and velvety texture.

  - *Thick-thin*: Alternates between very thick and thin sections, which lends a bumpy look to knitted fabric.

  - *Railroad ribbon*: Has tiny "tracks" of fiber strung between two parallel strands of thread.

  - *Faux fur*: Fluffy fiber strands on a strong base thread of nylon resemble faux fur when knitted.

- **Specialty:** These traditional types of yarn create special looks in knitted items:

  - *Tweed*: Has a background color flecked with bits of fiber in different colors.

  - *Heather*: Blended from a number of different-colored or dyed fleeces, and then spun.

  - *Marled (ragg)*: A plied yarn in which the plies are different colors.

  - *Variegated*: Dyed in several different colors or shades of a single color.

The available combinations can also create a luxury in **nylon, cashmere and nylon**, or **merino, alpaca, possum and nylon, nylon, merino and angora**, or **buffalo undercoat with nylon and wool**.

The traditional wool choice contains several advantages as compared to the modern choices. Wool blend socks are not only warm but also not likely to stretch out of shape unlike the machine made.

The preference of the **superwash yarn** over that which needs hand washing is another choice to consider. Practically, superwash contains the added benefit of being softer than the usual choice of regular wool, which makes it the preferred material for a lot of knitters.

Other wool options available include wonderful fibers like **cotton, bamboo, soy, sea cell, microfibers and viscose**. These are the preferred yarns for most knitters due to climate or sensitivity of the skin for the simple reason that they just love them on how they feel, look and wear.

Ideally, you will likely require sock yarn that is typically composed of 25% polyamide and 75% superwash wool. The wool enhances warmth in your socks even at times when the weather is damp. Superwash implies that that wool is treated with chemicals, which allows you to simply throw them in the washing machine. Your socks should not be tumble/dried but instead they should be dried flat which does not take a long time. Durability of the sock is enhanced by the polyamide, as poor wool wears through a lot more quickly.

It may surprise you to know that sock have been made from wool, cotton, acrylic, olefins, nylon, polyester, spandex, silk, cashmere and even bamboo! In fact, in the eighteenth century, the Greeks used to wear socks made from matted animal hair, which sounds terribly uncomfortable!

Standard Yarn Weight System

Yarn is categorized by weight, which is shown on the label. The *Craft Council of America* has organized a system to make it clear for knitters:

- **1** 1 or Super Fine   *(sock, baby and fingering yarn)*
- **2** 2 or Fine   *(baby and sport yarn)*
- **3** 3 or Light   *(light worsted and DK yarn)*
- **4** 4 or Medium   *(worsted, afghan and Aran yarn)*
- **5** 5 or Bulky   *(chunky, craft and rug yarn)*
- **6** 6 or Super Bulky   *(roving and bulky yarn)*

These numbers are designed to not only let you know **which yarn weights work best for specific patterns**, but also for **which knitting needles will be more effective**, as shown below. You can find out more information about the numbers related to the knitting needles in the <u>Sock Needles</u> chapter of this book.

KNITTING SOCKS FOR BEGINNERS

Yarn Weight:	0 Lace	1 Super	2 Fine	3 Light	4 Medium	5 Bulk	6 Super
Types of Yarn in Category.	Thread, Cobweb, Lace	Sock, Baby.	Sport, Baby	DK, Light, Worsted.	Worsted, Afghan.	Chunky, Craft, Rug.	Bulky, Roving.
Knit Gauge Range in Stockinet Stich to 4 inches.	30 – 40 sts	27 – 32 sts	23 – 26 sts	21 – 24 sts	16 – 20 sts	12 – 15 sts	6 – 11 sts
Recommended Needle in Metric Size Range.	1.5 – 2.25mm	2.25 – 3.25mm	3.25 – 3.75mm	3.75 – 4.5mm	4.5 – 5.5mm	5.5 – 8mm	8mm and larger
Recommended Needle in US Size Range.	000 – 1	1 – 3	3 – 5	5 – 7	7 – 9	9 – 11	11 and more
Crochet Gauge Range in Single Crochet to 4 inch.	32 – 42 double crochets	21 – 32 sts	16 – 20 sts	12 – 17 sts	11 – 14 sts	8 – 11 sts	5 – 9 Sts
Recommended Hook in Metric Size Range.	Steel 1.6 – 1.4mm	2.25 – 3.5mm	3.5 – 4.5mm	4.5 – 5.5mm	5.5 – 6.5mm	6.5 – 9mm	9mm and larger
Recommended Hook in US Size Range.	Steel 6, 7, 8 Regular Hook b-1	B-1 to E-9	E-4 to 7	7 to I-9	I-9 to K10½	K10½ to M-13	M13 and larger

Yarn For Socks – What's Available

In the majority of cases, **socks will be made with a mixture of wool** blend **or** wool, although cotton and **cotton wool blends** also work very well. In addition to warmth, wool absorbs moisture from the skin thereby making it an extremely suitable fiber for socks. Wool usually has an elasticity that is natural, which allows socks to hold their shape well and fit snugly.

That being said, you should remember, when making woolen socks, it is **important to select wool yarn, which contains a fraction of some nylon** that will add strength to those areas, which will tend to wear like toes and heels. If that isn't possible, **you can always add a reinforcement yarn** which is a thin blend of wool and nylon. This can be added to pure wool when knitting the sock areas requiring additional strength.

For warm weather socks, cotton is not only cool but also ideal due to its lack of elasticity. A useful tip to remember when considering cotton socks, choosing a pattern that features a ribbed cuff will ensure a more snug fit. **Socks may be made with any yarn weight** even if the choices that are most common are *sock weight* or *fingering, sport weight* or *DK* and also *worsted weight*. Just like any item that is knit, if the yarn is thick, the needles required will be large and the stitches fewer for the desired circumference to be achieved for the gauge swatch.

The gauge swatch is designed to test the yarn and a needle you're using, to make sure that the end result of your knitting project – in this case socks – is going to end up the desired size. It is worked out by the ***number of stitches per inch*** and is measured by counting the number of stitches over several inches, then dividing this by the number of inches in the width of the sample.

It is recommended to make a gauge swatch before starting a knitting project, and details on how to do this will be included in the pattern. (A step-by-step guide for creating a gauge swatch will be in a later chapter of this book.) This will ensure that the finished piece will be the size you want it to be, that the yarn and needle size you've selected are suitable, and it will make sure all the stitches you create are even.

The Fingering

Knitting socks with ***fingering yarn*** will have a gauge that is fine and will be very thin making the socks easy to wear with any shoe.

If you choose to work with fingering weight yarn, you'll require about 400 yards (365 meters) of it for an average pair of socks.

The Sport

The ***sport weight yarn or DK*** knitting yarn results in socks that are a bit heavier that can be worn with casual shoes.

You will require 350 yards (320 meters) of sports weight yarn for the average sized pair of socks.

The Worsted

KNITTING SOCKS FOR BEGINNERS

The type of socks made of the yarn known as **worsted-weight** are normally thick and very heavy. They are also referred to as *boot socks*.

You will require 280 yards (or 256 meters) of worsted weight yarn for the average sized pair of socks.

Selecting The Right Knitting Needle

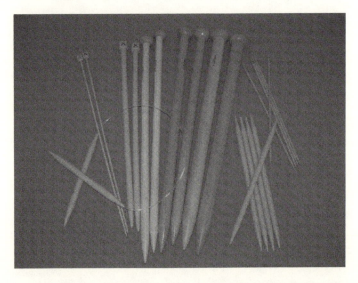

Selecting the right type of needle for knitting socks can be challenging as there are a lot of options available. However, it is often listed on a knitting pattern alongside the yarn to give the best results. You *can* choose to use a different yarn and needle size for a pattern, but you'll have to work on the gauge carefully to ensure you achieve the right sized socks as a result. It definitely isn't recommended for beginners to do this.

The Knitting Needle

It is worth noting that you will eventually decide on your own preference for knitting needles, so this guide is simply there to get you started

Remember **the size of needles will be determined by the weight of the yarn as well as the gauge**; however, the needle type will be upon you to choose. Needles may be made out of plastic, metal, nickel-plated, aluminum, walnut, cherry or rosewood and even bamboo. (When knitting was a relatively new concept, they used to use *bone* to make the needles!). Different people work better with different needles so if one type doesn't suit you, don't give up on knitting, and simply try a different material!

Plastic needles are not recommended for beginners because although they can blend very well, they can easily break. Beginners also need to avoid *aluminum needles* as they are very slippery and as such, stitches may easily fall off the needle. *Metal needles* are others that beginners should avoid since beginners will try to tightly hold their needles. Instead, a gentle needle should be used. **For the beginner, wood or bamboo materials are highly commendable**. Indeed, this is the needle that experts recommend for anybody. The *nickel-plated needles* are amazing and for those knitters who are experienced can readily enjoy the fast pace that they can get.

There are three basic types of knitting needles:

The Straight Type

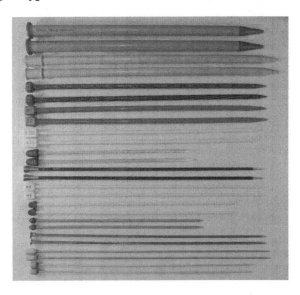

The knitting needle that is classic is straight and contains a single blunt end and a single pointed end. The straight needles vary in length ranging between 9 to 14 inches (22.8 to 35.5 cm) in length.

The Circular Type

A thin cable joins together two short needles that vary in length. As opposed to knitting back and forth, **these needles are used for knitting in a circular manner in the seamless round.**

The length of the longer needle is suitable for knitting wider items such as Afghans. Scarves can also be knit with the circulars, since the two ends of the circulars can be used to get back and forth. The scarf can be left to loosely hang on the cable when not knitting and you therefore need not worry about the stitches slipping off. As previously stated, circular needles are often used when knitting socks too, so throughout this book, you will become very familiar with them.

The Double Pointed Type

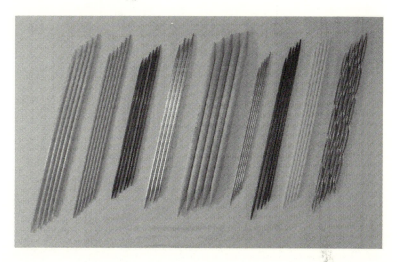

These types of needles have points on each of the ends. **They are usually designed for knitting a small round circumference like the sleeves, cuffs and socks.**

Experience shows that it is much simpler for beginners to **practice stitches by use of straight needles** as they are perfect for helping you get to grips with all of the necessary techniques. Once you get used to moving the needles from one hand to the other after every row, one may then consider **proceeding to the circular needles.**

Beginners are usually very fearful of the **double pointed needles**, but that shouldn't be the case because it does not take too much time for one to master them. They are great for particular techniques that produce beautiful results, so it's worth taking the time to practice with them until using them becomes natural.

When you purchase a set of **double pointed needles**, you will usually get a pack of five needles. Some people like to work with 4 needles, others like to use 5. You can practice with both methods to see which one suits you best.

Knitting Needle Sizes and Conversions

Metric Sizes, mm	UK Sizes	US Sizes
2.0	14	0
2.25	13	1
2.75	12	2
3.0	11	-
3.25	10	3
3.5	-	4
3.75	9	5
4.0	8	6
4.5	7	7
5.0	6	8
5.5	5	9
6.0	4	10
6.5	3	$10^{1/2}$
7.0	2	-
7.5	1	-
8.0	0	11
9.0	00	13
10.0	000	15
12.0	-	17

KNITTING SOCKS FOR BEGINNERS

16.0	-	19
19.0	-	35
25.0	-	50

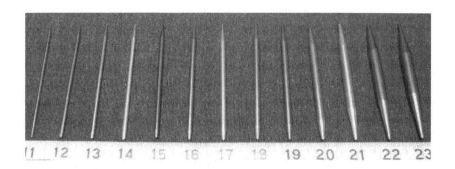

2 Ways To Hold Needles And Yarn

The next thing you need to know is **how to hold your selected knitting needles and yarn correctly.** Eventually you'll adapt and develop your own way of doing things, but it's always great to have a place to start.

You hold the right hand needle **as if it were a pencil.** When starting your knitting and working the first few rows, pass the knitted piece over the right hand between the thumb and index finger. As the work progresses, let your thumb slide under the knitted piece, grasping the needle from below – as shown above.

Hold the left hand needle over its top, using the thumb and index finger to control the tip of the needle.

KNITTING SOCKS FOR BEGINNERS

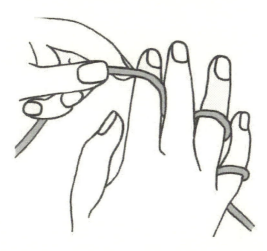

You hold the yarn in your right hand, passing it under your little finger, then around the same finger, over the third finger, under the centre finger and over the index finger. Use your index finger to pass the yarn round the needle tip. The yarn circled around the little finger controls the yarns tension.

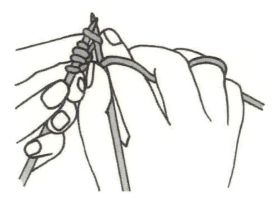

Alternatively, you can hold the yarn in your right hand and pass it under the little finger, over the third finger, under the centre finger and over the index finger. Use your index finger to pass the yarn to the needle tip. The tension is controlled by gripping the yarn in the crook of the little finger.

If you are left-handed, all you need to do is turn this around, so that the needle in you left hand is the one to do the majority of the work.

UNDERSTANDING PATTERNS

The first thing you need to know about knitting patterns is the information they contain. They will **always contain the following details**:

- *Skill level* – this is generally one of the very first things you'll see after the pattern name and picture. This information is useful to know as it will allow you to see if it's achievable. Sometimes this will be recorded as numbers 1 – 4 with one being the easiest.

- *Size* – this is especially important for garments.

- *Gauge* – this gives you the number of stitches per inch. The more you knit, the more this information will become vital to you.

- *Pattern information* – this section will give you the details of everything you need to *complete* the pattern. It'll let you know what yarn, needles and other equipment you need. Although you don't have to follow this exactly, it's best to stick closely to the sizes suggested so that the pattern will turn out as you want it.

- *Pattern abbreviations* – at a first glance, knitting patterns can seem very complex as they're written in abbreviations – and when you don't know what these mean, they can seem like a strange language. At the end of this guide there is a table of all of the standard abbreviations you are likely to come across.

Knitting patterns also have *specific terminology*, and this can vary from UK to US patterns, so it is best to be aware of these so there is no confusion:

UK	US
Tension	Gauge
Cast on	Bind on
Cast off	Bind off
Stocking stitch	Stockinette stitch
Moss stitch	Seed stitch

So now that you've seen all the abbreviations and terminology, it is time to look at an example line from a pattern.

*Row 1: *K2, P2; rep from * across, end K2.*

Which means you will knit the first two stitches, then purl the next two stitches; then knit 2, and purl 2 (don't worry, these stitches will be explained later), again, and repeat the steps following the asterisk all across the row until the last two stitches which you will knit. If you break the row down in this way, you'll find it very easy to get to grips with a knitting pattern.

A knitting pattern may ask you to knit in **rows or rounds**. Of course, this will determine which needles you use. *Straight needles* are suited to back and forth rows, and *circular and double pointed needles* are best for knitting rounds.

KNITTING CHARTS

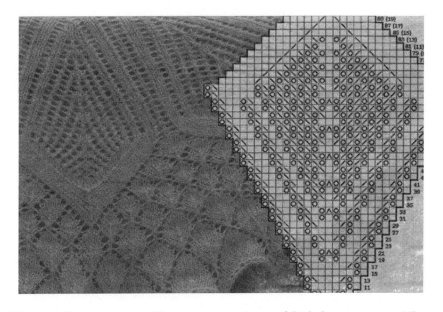

Knitting charts are **graphic representations of knitting patterns**. They also illustrate exactly how the item will look once it has been knit, giving the user the advantage of being able to identify any mistakes quickly.

In a knitting chart, each square represents a stitch, similar to the way that each abbreviation in text instructions does. Before starting working from a knitting chart, you should **familiarize yourself with the meanings of the symbols used**.

Below is an example:

key and abbreviations

☐ k - knit

○ yo - yarn over

⧄ k2tog - knit 2 together

⧅ ssk - slip, slip, knit - slip 1 knitwise, slip 1 knitwise, put 2 slipped sts back on LH needle and k2tog through back loops

▲ sl1-k2tog-psso - slip 1 knitwise together, knit 2 together, pass slipped st over

chart: gothic lace
Repeat rows 1-12

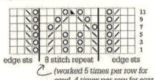

These charts can either show all of the rows, or sometimes they only show the 'right side' of the work. If the latter is the case, text instructions will also be included for how to work the **'wrong side' rows**.

all rows

chart: gothic lace
All rows shown

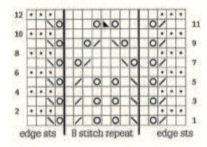

RS rows only

chart: gothic lace
Right-side rows shown, Wrong-side rows omitted.
All WS (even numbered) rows:
k3, purl to last 3 sts, k3

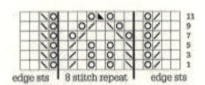

If the chart is **'right side'**, you will typically work the stitches one at a time from right to left. The instructions for the 'wrong side' will be written next to the chart, as shown below:

RS rows only ::: read from right to left and from bottom to top of chart

chart: gothic lace
Right-side rows shown, Wrong-side rows omitted.
All WS (even numbered) rows:
k3, purl to last 3 sts, k3

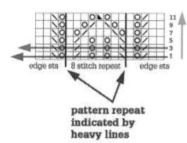

pattern repeat indicated by heavy lines

Row 1: k2, k2tog, yo, k1, *(edge stitches)* then start repeating pattern:
[ssk, k1, yo, k1, yo, k2tog, k1] repeat to last 4 sts,
yo, ssk, k2 *(edge sts)*

Row 2: *(not shown on chart) ... follow text instructions*
k3, purl to last 3 sts, k3

Row 3: k2, k2tog, yo, k1, *(edge stitches)* then start repeating pattern:
[ssk, k1, yo, k1, yo, k2tog, k1] repeat to last 4 sts,
yo, ssk, k2 *(edge sts)*

and so on and so forth...

If the knitting chart shows both the 'right' and 'wrong' side of the knitting project, you will work the 'right side' instructions from right to left, and the 'wrong side' instructions from left to right. By looking at the chart as a picture of the finished cloth, it will start to make sense as you progress.

START KNITTING

Now that we have had a look at patterns, and you've seen all of the abbreviations that are involved with knitting, **it's time to learn the stitches involved**. This chapter will show you exactly how to do them, with step-by-step guides and pictures.

The first step involved in knitting is making a **slip knot** and then **casting on**. This guide will help you with this.

Slip Knot

1. Start by making a loop with the yarn.

2. Bring the yarn through the loop, creating another loop with a knot at the end.

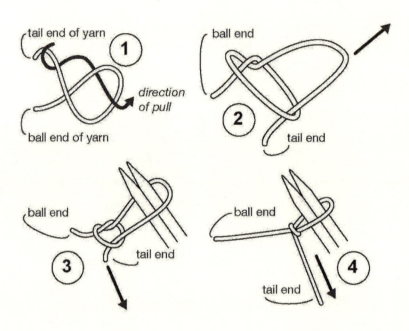

Cast On

After you have created the slip knot, you will need to cast on. This is effectively the first stitch to get you going. You may already know that this is something you need to do, but did you know that there are actually 4 different ways of doing this?

Single Cast On

1. Slide slip knot onto needle. Pull yarn to tighten knot.

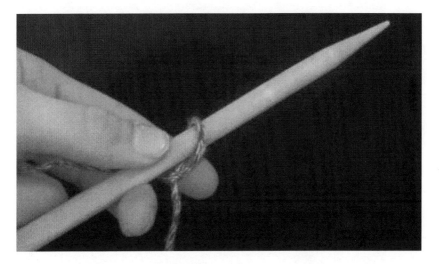

2. Wrap the working yarn (yarn connected to the ball of yarn) around your thumb so you have a loop around your thumb.

3. Bring the needle under and up through the loop around your thumb.

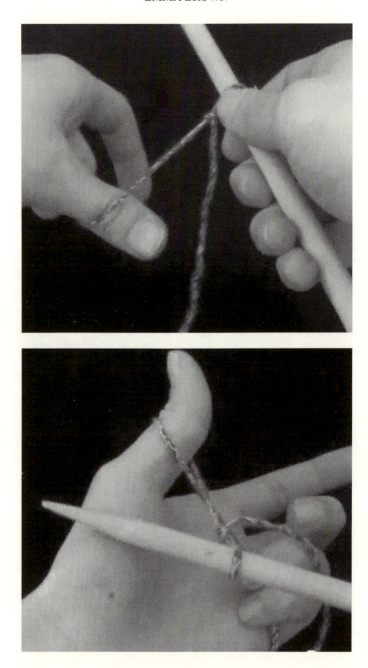

4. Remove your thumb from the loop and pull the yarn.

KNITTING SOCKS FOR BEGINNERS

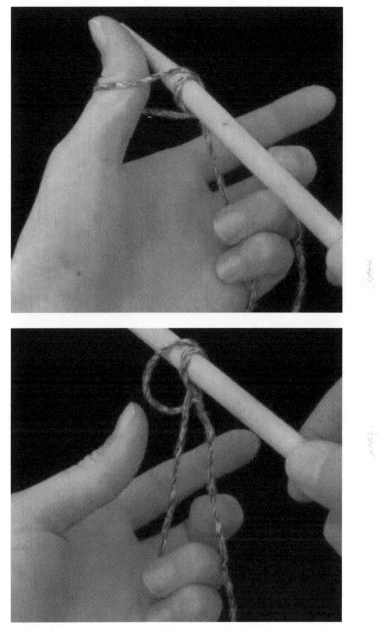

5. Continue from step 2 until you have desired number of stitches casted on.

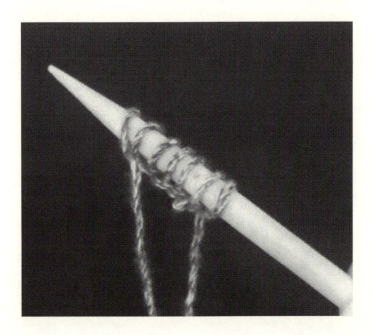

Longtail Cast On

Before you start to cast on, leave a tail at the end of the yarn. The length of the tail depends on the number of stitches you want to cast on. If you want to cast on 10 stitches leave about a foot of yarn for the tail.

1. Drape the tail over your thumb and pointer finger on your left hand.

2. Catch it in between your pointer and middle finger.

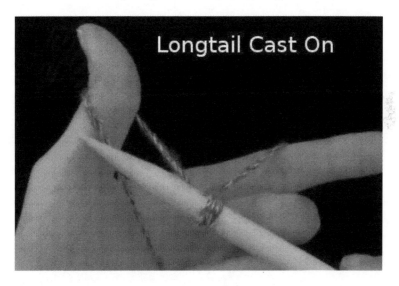

3. Catch the yarn connected to the ball against your palm with your pinky and ring fingers.

4. Take the needle in your right hand. Place it on top of the yarn between your thumb and pointer finger.

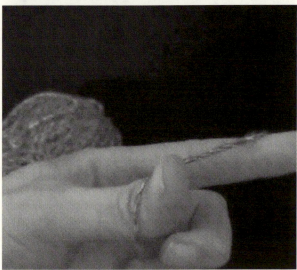

5. Draw the yarn towards you with the needle. You should see a loop of yarn around your thumb.

6. Bring the needle under the outer piece of yarn next to your thumb and up through the loop.

7. Bring the needle back towards your pointer finger.

KNITTING SOCKS FOR BEGINNERS

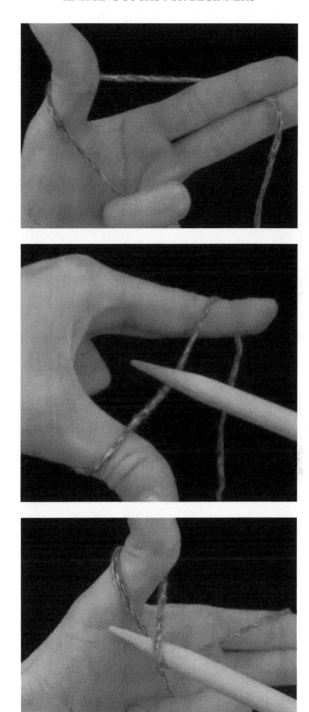

8. Bring the needle over the yarn connected to your pointer finger and then under back towards the thumb.

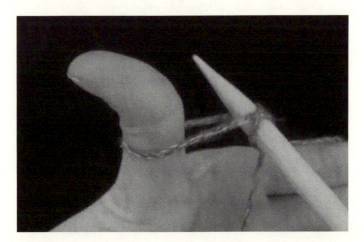

9. Drop the head of the needle back down through the loop around your thumb.

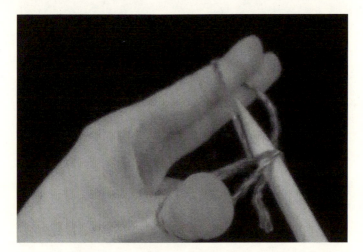

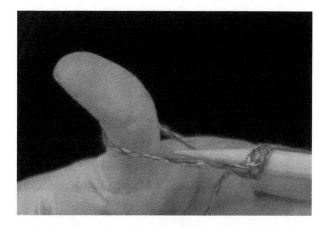

10. Release your thumb from the loop and pull the yarn.

11. Repeat from step 6 until you have the desired number of stitches casted on.

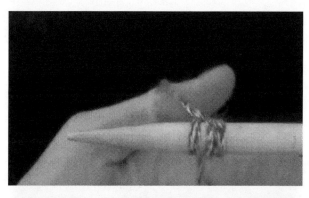

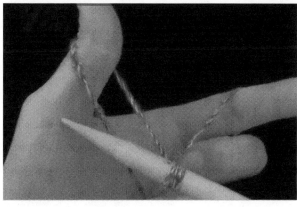

Knit Cast On

1. Make a slip knot and put it on your needle. Hold this needle in your left hand and take the second needle in your right hand.

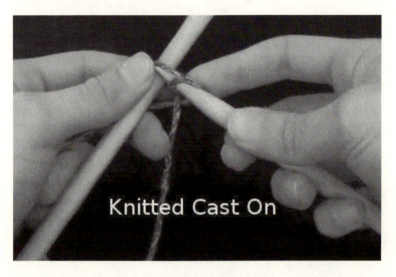

2. Pass the needle in the right hand through the loop on the left needle and bring the right needle under the left needle.

3. With your left hand, wrap the working yarn around your left hand needle.

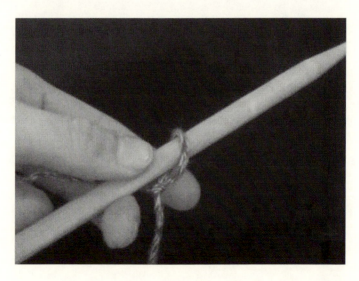

4. Bring the right needle back through the loop on the left needle.

5. Now you have a loop around your right needle. Turn the loop and drop it on to the left needle and release the right needle from the loop.

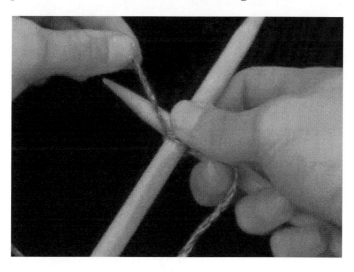

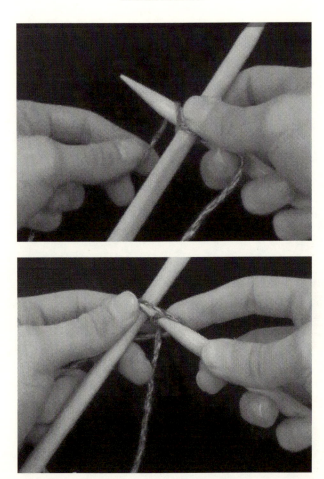

6. Pull the yarn and you have two stitches casted on.

7. To continue, repeat from step 2.

Cable Cast On

1. For the first two stitches, use instructions for knitted cast on.

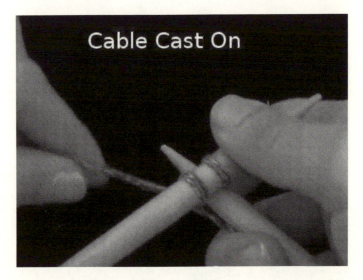

2. Once you have two stitches casted on. Take your right needle and put it in between the two stitches by bringing it under the left needle and through the yarn that connects the two stitches.

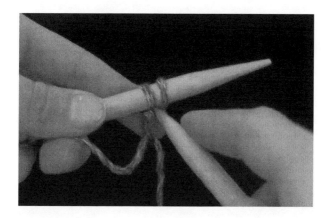

3. Wrap the working yarn around the right needle.
4. Bring the right needle back through the loops.

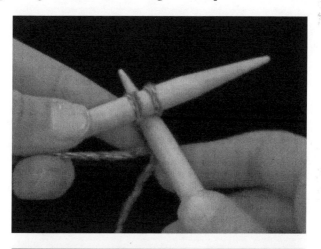

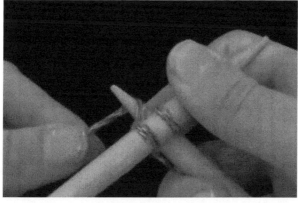

5. Now you have a loop around your right needle. Turn the loop and drop it on to the left needle and release the right needle from the loop.

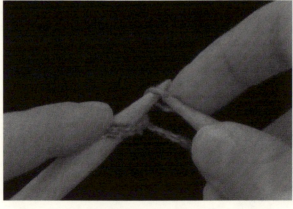

KNITTING SOCKS FOR BEGINNERS

6. Pull the yarn. You should have two stitches casted on.

7. To continue, repeat from step 2.

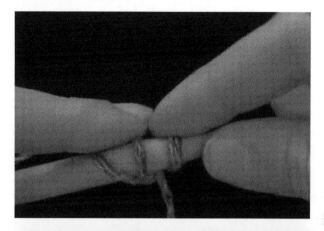

Knitting Gauge

Knitting a gauge swatch is so important as it helps you determine if the equipment you're using to knit with will create an end project that is the size you desire. Missing out this step can result in the whole project coming out entirely the wrong size. ***To complete the gauge, follow these steps:***

- ***Stitches*** – cast on the stitches required. It is normally 4 inches, plus 6 more stitches. So, for example. If the gauge is given as 18 stitches and 22 rows over 4 inches, cast on 24 stitches.

- ***Rows*** – work in the stitch pattern specified for the number of rows required to make 4 inches, plus 6 rows. Using the gauge specifications from the example above (18 stitches and 22 rows over 4 inches), you work in the given pattern of 28 rows.

- ***Bind Off*** – finish the project and bind off loosely, cut the yarn leaving an 8 inch tail.

- ***Measure*** - you'll then want to measure the swatch to check if the right number of stitches created the right size swatch. If not, you will need to change the needle size or yarn or the end result will be wrong. If you need more stitches per inch, you need smaller needles or thinner yarn and if you need less stitches per inch, you'll want to change to bigger needles or thicker yarn.

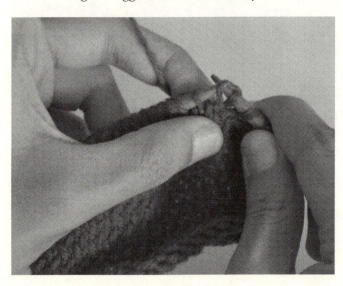

KNITTING SOCKS FOR BEGINNERS

FINISHING YOUR PROJECT

You have to Cast/Bind Off your knitting properly to prevent your work from unraveling. Here is a great step-by-step guide for doing this in the most effective way possible:

Step 1: Knit the first 2 stitches of the row.

Step 2: Insert the left needle into the first stitch on the right needle.

Step 3: Pull the first stitch on the right needle over the second stitch and off the right needle.

The second stitch will now be the only stitch on the right needle.

Step 4: Knit the next stitch on the left needle so that there are now 2 stitches on the right needle.

Repeat steps 2 and 3 until the end of the row.

When all stitches in the row have been bound off, cut a tail at least 4" long (or as long as the pattern specifies) and pull this tail through the last stitch, pulling to secure the work.

STITCHES

This chapter is going to look at a few of the stitches and techniques that will help you when it comes to knitting socks. It has step-by-step instructions to ensure you don't struggle with them.

Flat Knitting

Flat knitting is the process of **knitting in rows, where you periodically turn the work.** There is a 'right side' and a 'wrong side' of the project. Once you have Cast On, you immediately start to knit the next row from the pattern. Here is a guide to start flat knitting:

Step 1: Place your right needle behind the left needle.

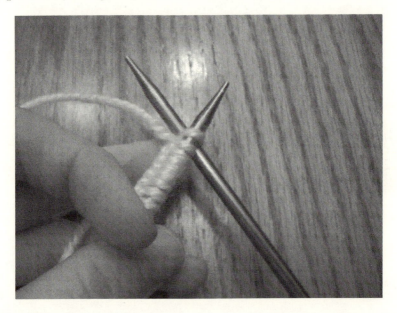

Step 2: Wrap the yarn counter clockwise around the right needle, and behind the left needle.

Step 3: Pull the yarn through the loop so it is on the right needle (like above).

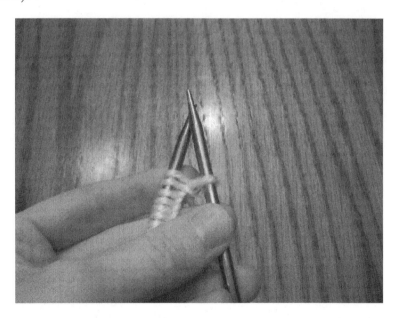

Step 4: Here's where it gets different. Push the first stitch on the left needle off of the needle completely.

Step 5: Now you'll have less stitches on the left needle, and one on the right.

Step 6: Continue this same method down the row.

Step 7: Once all of the stitches are off of the left needle and on the right needle, that row is done.

Step 8: For the next row, move what was your right needle to your left hand now, and your left needle to your right hand (flip them). The needle with the stitches on it will always start off in your left hand.

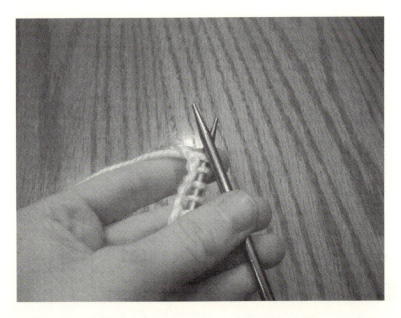

Step 9: Continue stitching the next row as you did the first.

Step 10: When you have the next row done, you will begin to see the pattern forming.

KNITTING SOCKS FOR BEGINNERS

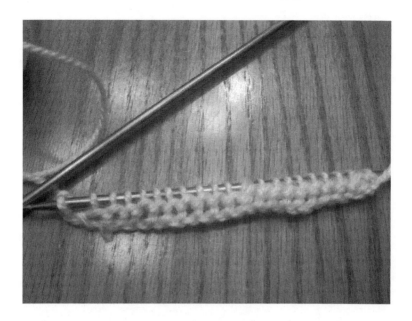

Circular Knitting

Circular knitting – or **knitting in the round** – is a **form of knitting that creates a seamless tube**. Using circular knitting needles, the yarn is cast on and the circle of stitches is joined. This type of knitting is perfect for creating socks, mittens or bigger projects such as sweaters.

Here are the instructions:

If you don't join the ends, you can use your circular needle to knit flat pieces, just like you'd knit on conventional needles. Because of the long connector between the needles, you can knit large items like afghans and not have to join then.

You can also knit in the round on your circular needles. When you do, you'll find that the right side of the work is facing towards you, which can make patterns easy to see.

You cast on to your circular needle in exactly the same way that you cast onto straight needles.

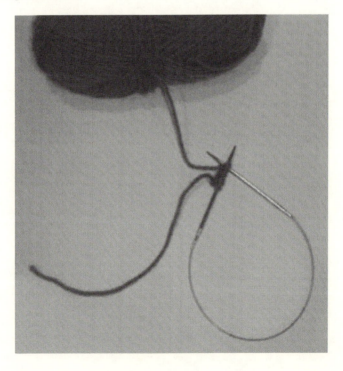

Continue to cast on until you have the number of stitches required for your pattern. You'll find that the circular needle is now full.

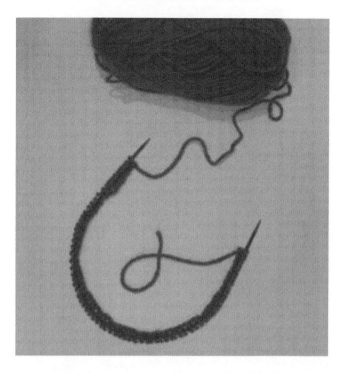

It is extremely important when joining your work that it is not twisted around the needle! If your piece is twisted, you will end up having to rip it out. To join, hold your needle so that the yarn is coming from the right. When you are knitting in the round, it is a good idea to use a stitch marker to know where your piece began - slip one onto your needle now if you will be using one. Place your knitting on a flat surface and carefully turn your cast-on stitches so that they are all facing in the same way (in our example, they are facing to the bottom and inside of the needle.)

Then insert the right needle into the first stitch that you cast on and knit the stitch. Be sure to pull the first stitches tight so you don't get a gap where the rounds join.

Continue to knit – you'll find that the 'right' side is always on the outside and that, as your work grows, that patterns are easy to see!

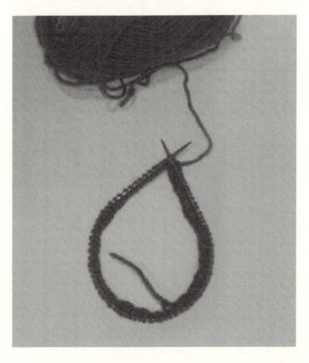

The Purl Stitch

The Purl Stitch is generally the second stitch that knitters learn. It's primarily thought of as a **backwards stitch**. Always remember to keep the working yarn in front of your needles. If you're switching between knit and purl stitches, you will move your working yarn from the back of the work to the front of the work, between the needles, to prepare for a purl stitch.

Step 1: You must first cast on or pick up stitches to have a foundation of stitches on your left needle.

Step 2: Holding your working yarn to the front and keeping yarn tensioned over your left index finger, insert the needle from back to front through the first loop on the needle. Keep the left needle under the right needle and the yarn to the front of the work. With your left index finger, bring the working yarn over the top to the bottom over the right needle to create a loop.

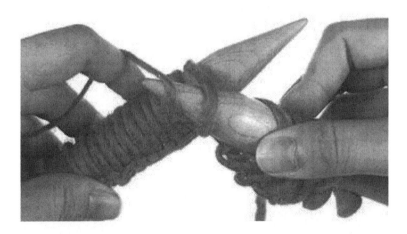

Step 3: Pull the loop on the right needle back out through the stitch on the left needle.

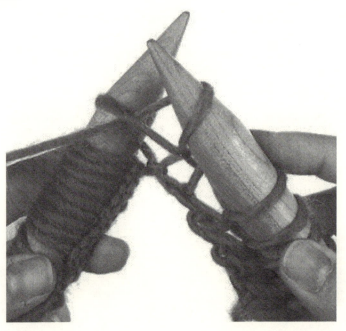

Step 4: Moving your right needle, slip the stitch off of the left needle. This completes a purl stitch. Continue to make as many purl stitches in the row as desired.

Kitchener Stitch

Here is a great set of instructions for this stitch.

Hold the needles parallel with the tips pointing in the same direction and the wrong (purl) sides facing inwards.

Now you'll need to "set up" for grafting by performing the following two steps one time:

Insert the threaded tapestry needle into the first stitch on the needle closest to you as if to purl and pull it through, leaving the stitch on the needle.

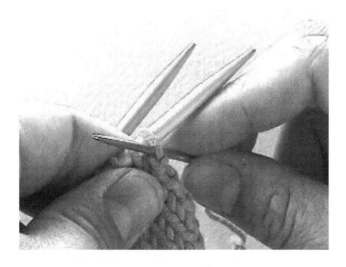

Then insert the needle into the first stitch on the back needle as if to knit, leaving the stitch on the needle. Pull the yarn through.

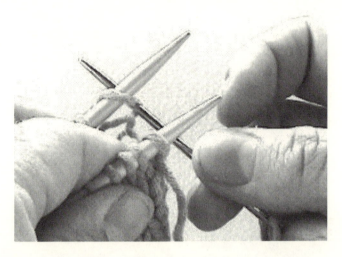

These first two steps are preparatory and are only done once.

Now let's get down to some serious kitchenering - the following four steps are the ones you will repeat until you've worked every stitch on the needles. I usually chant to myself "knit, purl -- purl, knit" while grafting and you'll soon see why.

Step 1: Insert the needle into the first stitch on the front needle as if to knit, while slipping it off the end of the needle.

Step 2: Insert the needle into the next stitch on the front needle as if to purl, but this time, leave it on the needle. Gently pull the yarn through.

Step 3: Insert the needle into the first stitch on the back needle as if to purl, and slip it off the end of the needle.

Step 4: Insert the needle into the next stitch on the back needle as if to knit, and leave it on the needle. Pull the yarn through.

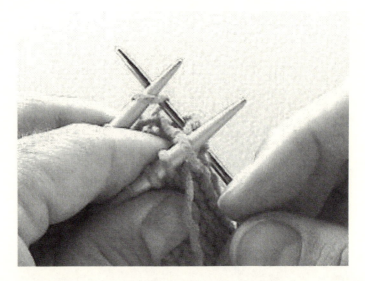

Repeat steps 1-4 over and over again. After you've worked a couple of inches, pause [being sure to complete step 4 so you'll know where to begin again] and tighten up the stitches using the end of the tapestry needle to tug at each loose loop in turn, working from the beginning of the join towards the last stitches worked. I find I get a nicer final result when I pull the yarn lightly through the stitches during the process of grafting and then adjust the tension on the yarn to match the gauge of the knitting as closely as possible afterwards.

KNITTING SOCKS FOR BEGINNERS

Rib Stitch

The ribbing stitch looks great whether it's done in one block solid color, or a few colors. It's often used to create afghans, scarves and garments.

The ribbing stitch uses two stitches – a knit stitch and a purl stitch. Start by knitting two stitches. Bring the yarn from the back of your work between the needles to the front. Now purl two stitches. Bring the yarn to the back of your work between the needles. Knit two stitches. Continue to knit two stitches, purl two stitches until you reach the end of the row or until the pattern instructs you to do something different.

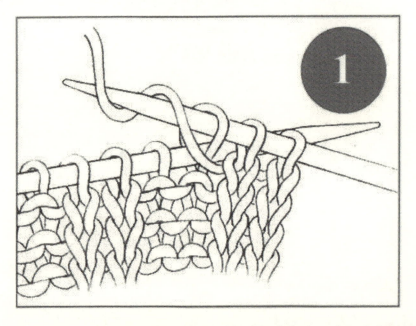

On subsequent rows, knit the knit stitches (V stitches) and purl the purl stitches (bump stitches) Remember to have the working yarn in BACK when you knit and in FRONT when you purl.

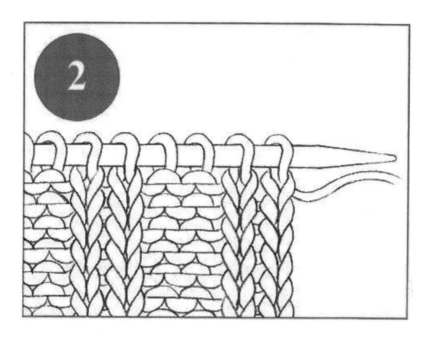

Stockinette Stitch

Here is a step-by-step guide for Stockinette stitch:

Step 1: Cast on stitches using your preferred cast-on method.

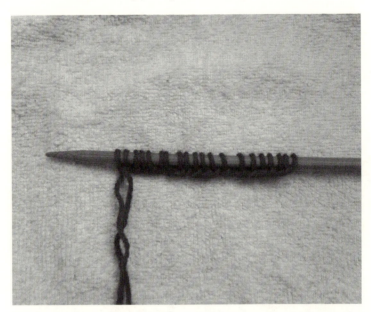

Step 2: Purl all stitches.

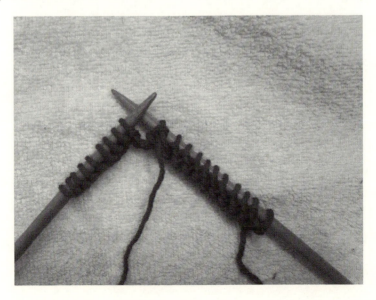

Step 3: Knit all stitches.

Repeat Steps 2 and 3 for as long as desired.

This is the right side of the fabric.

Now, for this swatch, I used straight pins to hold the ends down because as you can see in the next photo, the nature of stockinette stitch fabric is to curl. Even after a good wet blocking, you will find that the sides of the fabric will curl.

You will come across other stitches with knitting sock patterns, but these basics will get you started. Once you have gotten to grips with these, learning other stitches will be much simpler as you already have some under your belt.

Slip Slip Knit (SSK)

You will quite often come across a Slip Slip Knit (SSK), in knitting sock patterns, so here is the step-by-step guide on how to do this:

1. Slip the first stitch on the left-handed needle (as if to knit) to the right-handed needle without actually knitting it.

2. Do the same with the next stitch.

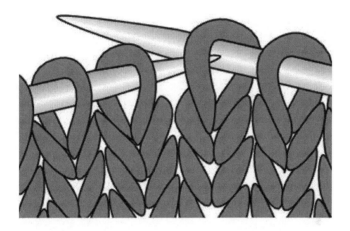

3. Insert the left-handed needle into the front loops of these stitches (left to right).

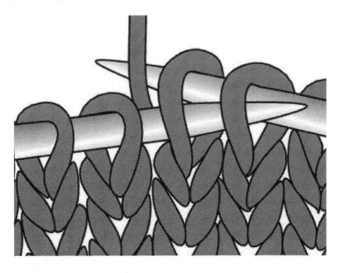

4. Wrap the yarn in the usual way around the right-handed needle and knit the 2 slipped stitches together.

To work an ssk on the purl side, follow these steps:

1. Slip the first stitch on the left-handed needle (as if to knit) to the right-handed needle.

2. Do the same to the next stitch.

3. Keeping the 2 slipped stitches facing in this direction, transfer them back to the left-handed needle.

4. Purl the 2 stitches together through the back loops.

KNITTING TECHNIQUES

There are also a few knitting techniques that will help you with you sock patterns. Practicing these will help you in the long run, because you're very likely to come across them.

Joining Yarn

At some point in your knitting, you will need to add a new ball of yarn. If you're completing a large project, it's likely you will need more than one ball. This is a demonstration on how to do this:

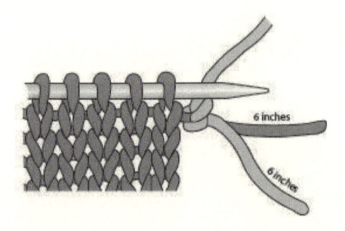

Step 1: Work a couple of stitches in from the end of your project. Leave 12 – 18 inches of your tail.

Step 2: Take the tail of the new ball of yarn and hold it with the tail from your project. Make sure the tails are going opposite directions from each other.

Step 3: Work a few more stitches holding both strands of yarn together.

Step 4: Continue working with the new strand, leaving 6 – 8 inches of your old tail

Note: **Be careful to work both strand together as one during the next row.**

When you ready, weave both tails into the project.

Increase & Decrease

Some knitting patterns require you to increase or decrease stitches to change the width of your knitting. Increasing is adding in a stitch, decreasing is taking one out. Below are a few ways to do this.

Increase Stitches

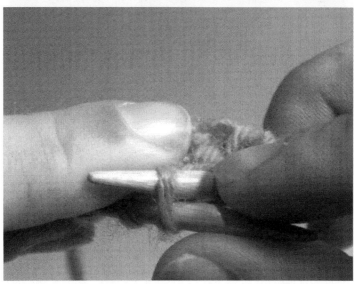

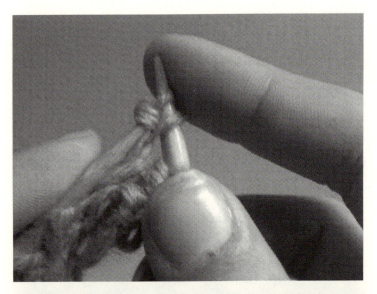

Increase Stitch: Basically, you are knitting two stitches like normal, but the first time you knit a stitch you do not slip the stitch off the left needle.

- Knit a stitch, but don't slip the stitch off your left needle

- Instead, bring your right needle through the top stitch on your left needle, and knit another stitch.

- Now remove the stitch from the left needle.

Increase: Yarn Over

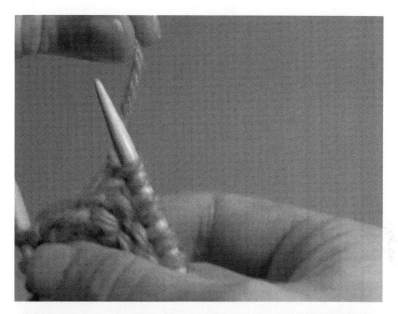

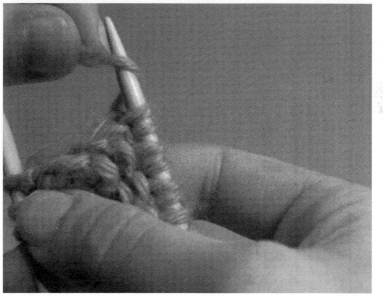

Yarn Over: this technique leaves holes in yarn. It is usually done for decorative stitches. When you want to leave an eyelet in your yarn use this technique.

- Knit a stitch

- Wrap yarn once around right needle to make an extra loop on right needle.

- Continue knitting.

Decrease Stitches

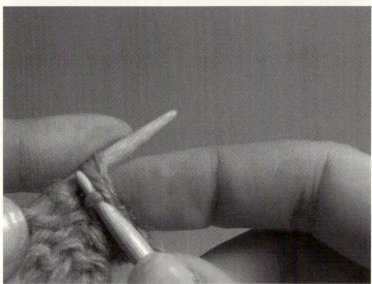

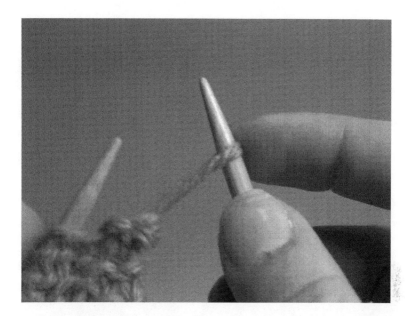

Knit Two Together: everything is the same as making a knit stitch, but instead of passing the needle through the top stitch on the left needle, pass the needle through the top two stitches and knit as if it were one stitch.

Decrease KRPR

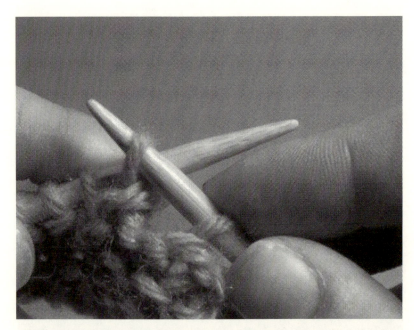

KRPR = Knit, Return Pass, Return

- *Knit* one stitch

- *Return* stitch you just knitted back on to the left needle

- Take the second stitch on left needle using your right needle and **pass** it over the top stitch on the left needle and off the needle.

- *Return* top stitch on left needle back to right needle.

Changing Color

Many patterns ask for a change in color of the yarn – or you may choose to do it yourself to add a unique quality to your projects. A guide for how to do this is presented below.

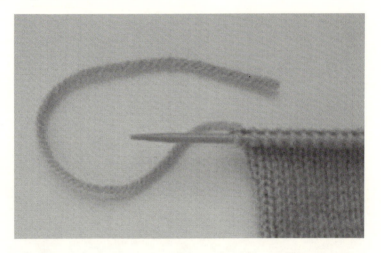

At the end of the row, cut the yarn leaving a tail about 20cm long.

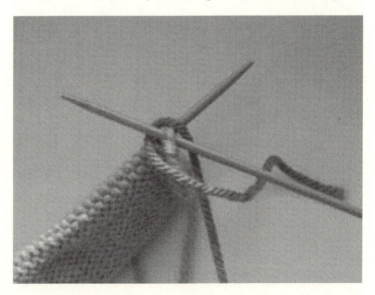

At the beginning of the next row, slip the tip of the right needle into the first stitch on the left needle in the usual way. Loop the new yarn around the tip of the right needle.

KNITTING SOCKS FOR BEGINNERS

Work the first three or four stitches on the row using the new yarn, keeping hold of the tails at the end of the row as you knit so that your stitches do not unravel. After knitting the few stitches, tie the tail ends in a knot to secure at the end of the row.

Now continue knitting the row as normal with your new color.

Sewing in Loose Ends

Sewing in the loose ends of your knitting can be done in many ways – eventually you will find your own preferred method. Here is a step-by-step guide to a few of these to get you started.

A one color garment presents no problem as to where to sew in the yarn. Unless you have some join in the fabric of the knitting, all the threads will be on an edge, and edges are where the seams or bands occur. These ends are easily sewn into the seams.

You can also make the ends vanish by using a sharp pointed needle with a large eye. Undo any loose knots you might have made when adding in a new end. Usually, there are two ends at one point. With one end, push the threaded needle through the edge of the rows that make the ridge of the seam. Pull the thread through and cut it off closely. Repeat with the second end in the opposite direction along the seam. Basically, you are burying the ends in the seam.

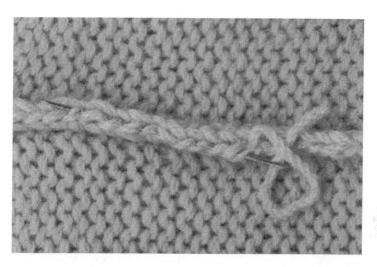

Sometimes you have a short end that will be impossible to thread into the needle and then sew in to the seam. Push the unthreaded needle along the seam starting from where the end is sticking out, then thread the end into the eye and pull the end through.

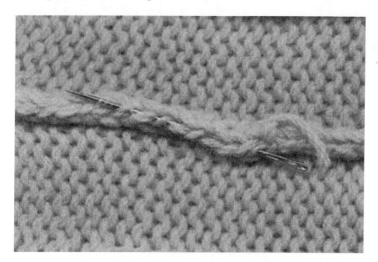

Seams should be as fine as possible so that they will have the same flexibility as the knitted fabric. For this reason, it is important to make sure that the ends don't add too much thickness to the seam. The ends will stay perfectly in place as long as you make sure that you have buried them adequately in the seam. Also, take the ends some distance along the seam. If they are too short, they could work their way out more easily. Don't weave an end around the edge stitches of the seam, it will always unweave with wear.

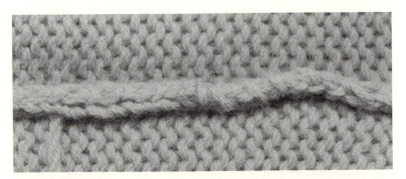

Don't sew any ends over and over the seam. This will only make a big lump that could stick out under the seam on the right side, and won't hold any better than using a sharp needle and sewing the thread firmly through the ridge of the seam.

If you have used two or more colors, sew the ends in to the matching colored seam. If you have sewn in the ends properly, you shouldn't even glimpse a sewn-in end on the right side, but this is extra insurance.

Color changes, patches or a knitted-in design result in ends located in the fabric of the garment. These should also be sewn in to the matching color on the wrong side, but now you don't have a seam to hide the ends.

Make a tiny stitch on the back at the base of the end, then carefully push the needle through matching stitches along the horizontal color change row, or vertically along the side of the color patch.

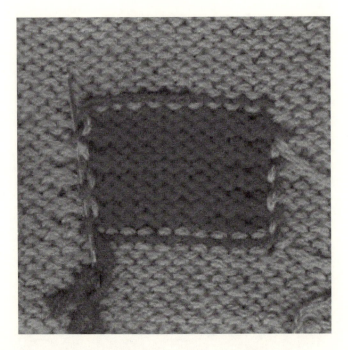

Matching the color will mean there is less of a chance that the ends will show through on the right side.

Dropped Stitches

It is inevitable that you will accidently drop a stitch at some point, so it's useful to know how to rectify this mistake. It doesn't matter where about you do it, there is a fix as shown below.

Down a Row – Knitwise

Insert your left needle through the front of the dropped stitch so it won't travel any farther.

Insert the left needle under the loose strand directly above the dropped stitch.

With the right needle, pull the dropped stitch over the strand and tip of the needle.

Now knit the stitch on the left needle.

Down a Row – Purlwise

Insert the left needle into the purl st.

Insert the left needle under the loose strand. It should now be to the right of the dropped stitch on the left needle.

With the right needle, lift the dropped stitch over the strand and the point of the needle.

Pull the strand through the stitch.

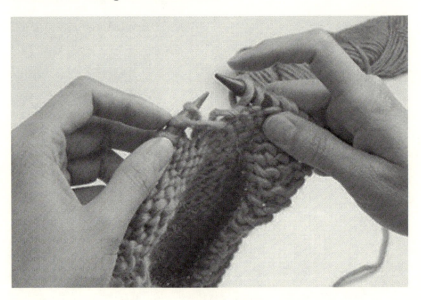

Transfer the stitch back to the left needle and purl it.

KNITTING SOCKS FOR BEGINNERS

Several Rows Down

Position your work so you're above and at the same vertical point as the dropped stitch on the knit side of your work. Pull the needles apart very gently, exposing the horizontal lines from each of the rows missing the stitch.

Look at your work carefully, and assess how many rows the stitch has fallen. The sample shows 4 loose strands, representing 4 rows.

With the crochet hook inserted into the dropped stitch, hook the strand right above the stitch and pull it through.

Pull next strand through, and repeat until all the stitches are picked up from the previous rows.

Repeat this process until you're at the same row as the needles. Place the last stitch on the left needle, and continue in the stitch pattern.

Tension

Controlling the tension in your yarn whilst knitting is a really useful skill to master as it will make everything else come much easier and many more of your projects will be successful. Practicing with the knitting gauge is the best way to do this.

First, try a few different needles of different material to get the gauge and tension that is best for your project. If your stitches are sliding off the needle willy-nilly, you might need to go down a size or two. If your stitches just won't budge, try a smoother material like aluminum.

Keep a loose grip on the yarn as you knit. Don't tug on the yarn as you complete each stitch. If you'd like your fabric to be more dense, go down a needle size or two rather than trying to knit tighter.

Maintain even tension by consciously focusing on your knitting rhythm for the first few minutes after you pick up your needles. Knitters who like to watch movies or listen as they knit find their tension getting too tight during a chase scene or too loose during a song and dance number. Commuter knitters find their tension changes from the ride to work and their ride home. Unless you like your knitting to be a diary of your day, pay attention to the way you begin to knit; that will keep your hands focused even while your eyes wander.

THE DOUBLE POINT AND CIRCULAR NEEDLE METHODS

The Double Pointed Needles

When knitting socks, you'll often work with double pointed and circular needles. This chapter gives you details on how to use these successfully.

With double point needles, the needles with the last and first cast-on stitches need to be used for joining the stitches. Care should be observed not to have the stitches twisted when joining them so as to knit the round. In case the stitches twist round the needle, you will not get the beautiful flat tube that you require for a sock and the flaw will be easily noticeable after knitting the first few rows.

A regular way of joining a circular knit on the double point needles is by holding the first and also the last needles together closely. Then, start to knit clockwise with an empty needle thereby offering little tugs to the first few stitches.

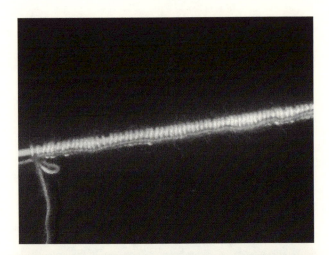
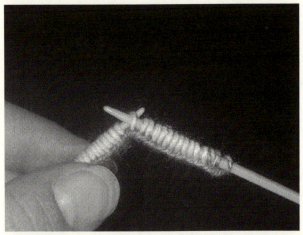
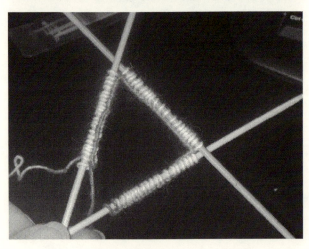

KNITTING SOCKS FOR BEGINNERS

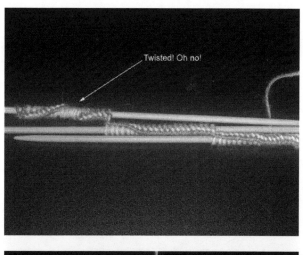

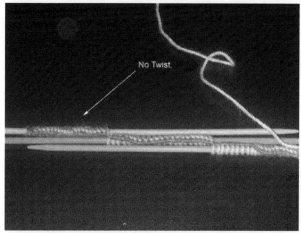

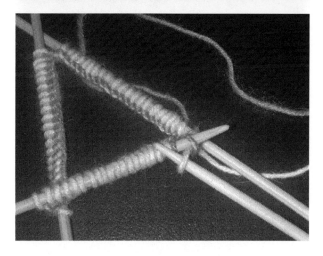

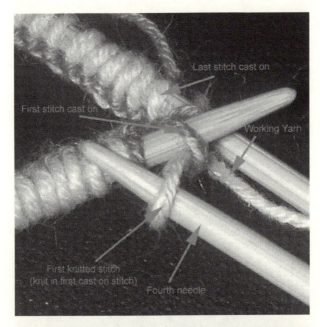

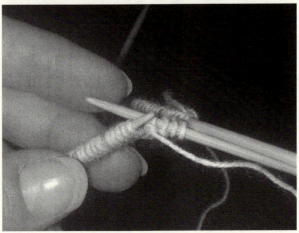

KNITTING SOCKS FOR BEGINNERS

Means Of Avoiding The Ladder Effect

One may encounter the *'ladder effect'* when you are using the double pointed needles. **The ladder effect is the gap created as you move the stitches from one needle to the next.** When the stitches may not be pulled adequately and tightly enough to have the needle shift overcome, one may obtain a stitch that is elongated. After making a number of rows, your stitches will start looking like a ladder.

This rather dreaded ladder effect can be easily avoided. **The most appropriate way to avoid it** is by moving to the next needle and offering an extra tug to the first two stitches as the yarn is wrapped thereby anchoring them to those stitches there before.

One should however not tug all the stitches since you could end up with a knit that is very tight and one can experience sore fingers. Moreover, it will be difficult in moving the stitches along the needle. Upon becoming comfortable with your knitting, you will discover a working tension that best works for you. At the same time, you do not have to pull too hard on your yarn. You need to be very gentle by loving your fibers.

The Stay Loose Method

Ensure that you cast loosely in order to ensure that the top is elastic in a nice manner for the foot to fit comfortably well around the calf. Ensure that you practice loosely by doing it with the same size of needle as used for the other part of the sock. The technique will enable you to have uniform stitches along the top of the sock.

In case you are still experiencing difficulties, ***the following tips will greatly assist you in staying loose***:

- Ensure that you hold two needles together and cast stitches on both of them. When the stitches are cast on all of them, remove one of the needles with care.

- You could also try to cast stitches on the needle that is two sizes larger than the pattern needles and let the cast on stitches be split onto the needles that are small before beginning and joining the socks.

- For the cast on, a larger needle should be used.

- After using a larger needle and joining, the first few rows need to be worked with a much larger sized needle.

- The stitches need not be tightened or pulled very closely together. A little space can be left between the cast on stitches thereby producing a top band that is elastic and also stitches which can be easily be worked with ease.

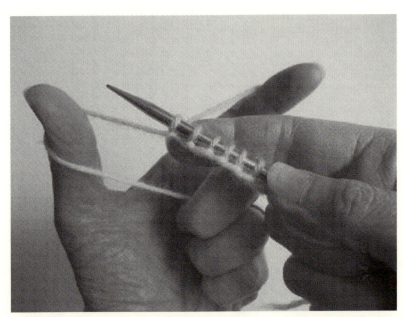
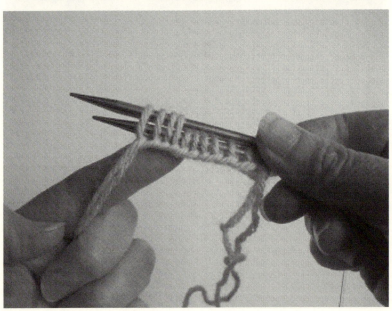

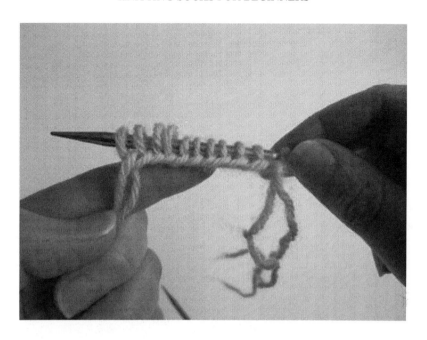

SOCK SIZING

Sock sizing is very much individualized the same way shoe sizing is. In fact, **the best approach to fitting a sock** is by measuring the wearer's foot from the heel's end to the toe's end and knit the length of the foot appropriately.

With socks bought from the stores, you need to choose ones which closely matches your foot. They are never *exact*. You can do a custom fit when you are knitting the socks yourself, making a much better product.

Before getting started, the following are **the measurements that are required**:

- **Leg Length.**

    This is the part at the back of the leg starting from the top most places where the sock should be to the heel's bottom.

- **Cuff Circumference**

    This is that part of the leg where the cuff needs to be.

- **Heel to Toe**

    This is the foot's bottom that starts from the heels' back to the area at the end of the large toe.

- **Toe Length**

    This refers to only the toes.

- **Foot Circumference**

    This is the part that is most wide for the foot where the base of the toes is.

Once you have all of these measurements for yourself – or whoever you're making the socks for, you'll be able to adapt patterns accordingly, making the end product of your knitting work much more likely to be successful.

CONSTRUCTING SOCKS

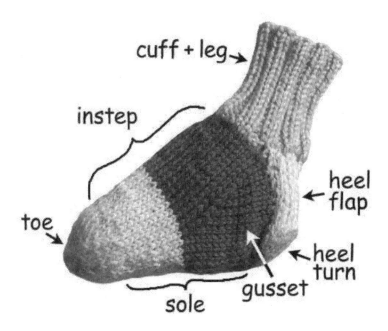

Most sock patterns will usually be knit on a set of four or even five needles that are double pointed. This will eliminate those seams at the toes and heels therefore making the socks much more comfortable for the wearer. The heels and toes are woven together by use of the *Kitchener stitch*. This is a type of stitch that resembles the knit stitch and will usually offer a neat seam that is not visible. This chapter will look at each of the segments of the sock individually.

The Cuff

Many of the sock knitters begin their work from the top to bottom by starting at the cuff. The preferred number of stitches will be cast to one needle and later equally divided to three or four sets of needles in rounds.

From the first round, this will help the stitches from twisting. For many of the socks, the number of stitches on the cuff will be equal to the foot's number of stitches after the heel and the completion of instep shaping.

More often than not, cuffs will start with measurements of 1½ /2½" or 3.5/6cm ribbing for additional elasticity at the sock's top even if some socks may get ribbed of the whole cuff's length. Others will get topped with a stitch pattern or lace and fail to feature any rib.

Below is a ***guide for sewing the sock cuff.***

Ribbing is a classic choice for sock cuffs and legs. Most knitters opt for 1 x 1 or 2 x 2 ribbing.

To work 1 x 1 ribbing, * knit 1, purl 1 * and repeat from * to * around the sock.

To work 2 x 2 ribbing, * knit 2, purl2 * and repeat from * to * around the sock.

You can switch from ribbing to Stockinette stitch after an inch or two for a cuff, or continue the ribbing straight down the leg for a close-fitting sock.

Add patterning

The leg is where many sock patterns incorporate different types of stitch patterns, such as cables, lace, or color work. The patterning may then continue down the front of the sock to the toe.

To incorporate a stitch pattern, figure out how many stitches the pattern requires. A lace pattern that has a 4-stitch repeat will fit nicely over any cast-on number from the chart, but it would be difficult to incorporate a 13-stitch repeat.

Many stitch patterns are presented through **the use of charts**. A chart is a pictorial representation of the knitted work viewed from the right (public) side. Each box in the chart represents 1 stitch in the knitting.

1. The chart begins in the bottom right-hand corner.

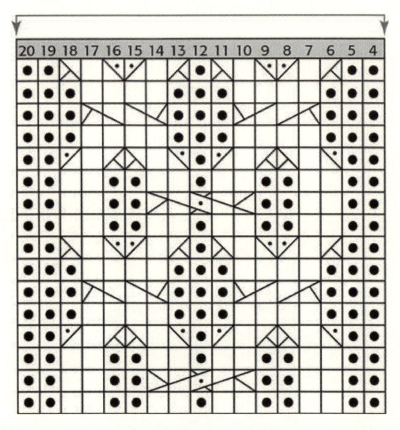

2. Read the line in the chart from right to left, repeating the entire box or an outlined portion as necessary, until you get to the end of the line. This is the end of the row.

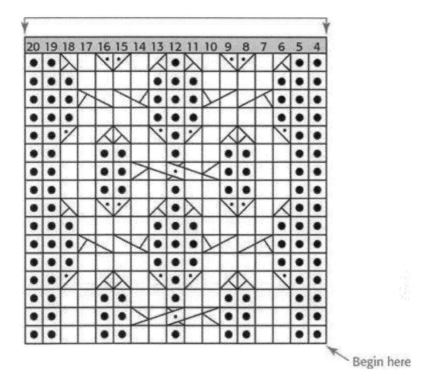

3. When **knitting in the round**, all rounds are read from right to left.

4. When **knitting flat**, wrong-side rows are read from left to right – so the direction of reading the chart alternates between right to left and left to right on each row.

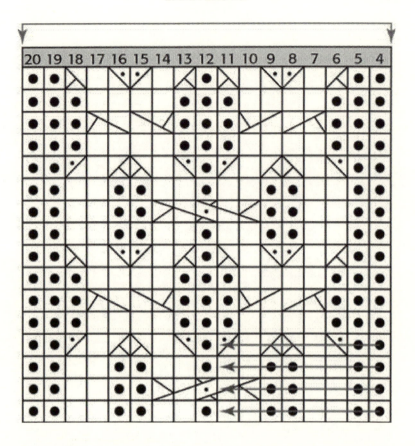

The Heel

After getting the desired length of the cuff, normally measurements of 5/7" or 12.5/17.5cm, the stitches number will be divided by two and the shift will surround the needles so that the needle's center heel begins at the cuff rounds. The instep stitches remaining which makes the foot's front will be divided into two onto both needles to get worked on later.

The heel will be straightly worked on with two needles, in rows back and forth till the preferred depth is reached. As is referred in most cases, the heel will then be turned or shaped into a V-shape with short rows or even a U curved shape. Since the techniques for turning the heel will vary, your pattern will describe the method suitable for the socks you desire to knit.

Here is a *guide for knitting the sock heel.*

Once the leg is complete, you knit the heel. It may look complicated, but only a few simple steps are involved. To shape the sock so that it fits around the curve of the foot, the gusset heel consists of three steps— knitting a heel flap, shaping the bottom of the heel, and decreasing for the gusset. The example sock contains 64 cast-on stitches.

Knit the heel flap

The heel flap is typically knit on half the total number of sock stitches and in a slipped-stitch pattern for thickness and durability. You knit it back and forth (not in the round) to produce a flap for the back of the heel.

1. Knit one needle (25%) of the sock's stitches as follows:

Row 1: * Slip 1 purlwise with yarn in the back, knit 1 *, rep from * to * across.

Example sock: Work 16 stitches in the pattern.

2. Turn the work so that the inside of the sock is facing you.

3. Work across two needles (50% of the sock's stitches) as follows, working all the stitches onto one needle:

Row 2: Slip 1 purlwise witn yarn in the front, purl across.

Example sock: Work 32 stitches in pattern.

4. Repeat rows 1 and 2 until the heel flap is square – work as many rows as there are stitches in the heel flap.

Example sock: The heel flap is 32 stitches wide and 32 rows long.

You can figure out how many rows of heel flap you've knit by counting the large chain stitches on either edge. You'll have half as many chain stitches as the number of heel flap stitches when the flap is done!

Turn the heel

Turning the heel involves the use of short rows to shape the "cup" at the bottom of the heel. Short rows are rows where you only work part of the stitches in the row, leaving some stitches to be worked later.

1. Knit across a prescribed number of stitches – usually a little more than half of the stitches.

Example sock: Knit 18 stitches.

2. Decrease by slip slip knit, then knit 1. Turn the work to the wrong side.

3. Slip 1 purlwise with the yarn in front, purl 5, purl 2 stitches together, purl 1.

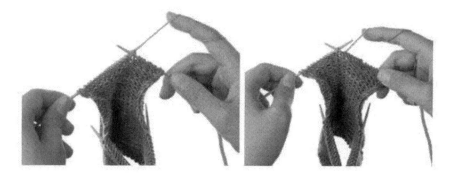

Socks with different stitch counts may prescribe a different number of purl stitches on this row.

4. Continue to work short rows as follows:

Row 1 (Right Side): Slip 1 purlwise, knit to 1 stitch before the gap created in the previous row, slip slip knit, knit 1, turn.

Row 2 (Wrong Side): Slip 1 purlwise, purl to 1 stitch before the gap, purl 2 stitches together, purl 1, turn.

5. Repeat these 2 rows until all the stitches of the heel flap are worked, ending with the RS facing for next row. If not enough stitches remain to complete the purl 2 stitches together, purl 1 at the end of the last Wrong Side row, work as purl 2 stitches together.

Example sock: 18 stitches remain.

For a deeper heel, work more rows in the heel flap before turning the heel. For each 2 additional rows you add to the heel flap, pick up an additional stitch on either side of the heel flap when preparing for the gusset.

Make the gusset

The gusset consists of two parts: picking up stitches to connect the heel flap with the rest of the sock and working decreases to shape the sides of the foot.

1. Knit across all heel stitches (example sock: 18), then pick up stitches with another double-pointed needle as follows:

Insert the tip of the right (empty) needle below both legs of the slipped-stitch column along the edge of the heel flap. Wrap the yarn around the needle as if you were knitting, then pull the new stitch through the work to create a new loop on the right needle.

2. Continue to pick up stitches along the edge of the heel flap, 1 stitch for each slipped stitch along the edge, until 18 stitches are picked up.

3. Knit across the instep stitches that were held during the knitting of the heel, continuing any pattern if you desire, then pick up 18 more stitches along the other side of the heel flap. Knit across the heel flap stitches—this needle is now called Needle 1 and is the first needle of the round.

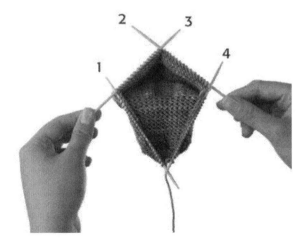

To prevent a hole at the top of the heel flap, you can pick up an extra stitch at the junction between the heel flap and the instep. Continue with the decreases as written until the original number of stitches remain.

4. Work decrease round as follows:

Needle 2: Knit to the last 3 stitches, knit 2 stitches together, knit 1.

Needle 3: Work across in pattern.

Needle 4: Knit 1, slip slip knit, knit to end of needle.

5. Knit 1 round even.

6. Repeat the last 2 rows until 64 stitches remain, or the original cast-on number.

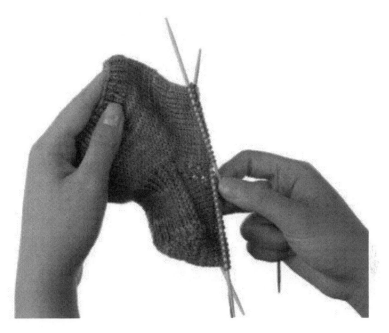

To prevent holes from forming at the top of the gusset, pick up an additional stitch at the very corner of the gusset where it meets the instep (top of the foot) on either side of the foot. Continue the decreases as given.

The Instep

In order to start working in rounds once more and to also have the instep joined to the heel, stitches are often knit and repositioned once more in order for the round to start at the heel's center which is the sole's foot. Stitches will be picked and knit alongside the heel's piece whereby the stitches will become part and parcel of the instep. In successive rounds, these stitches will become fewer on either foot's side and in most cases the first and third needles till it reaches the initial stitches number in the round. This consequently makes the instep to the shape of a wedge also referred to as a gusset. This fits in the wearer's foot since it decreases in width starting from the heel.

Below is a step-by-step **guide to knit the instep**.

The instep is knit on half of the total number of stitches, from the side edge of the heel down to the toe in the center of the leg piece. You work the top of the toe at the end of the instep, which you seam with the bottom of the toe after you finish knitting.

1. Work across the leg piece until 25% (16 stitches of a 64-st sock) of the stitches remain unworked. Place the remaining 25% of the stitches (16 stitches) on a holder to work later for the heel.

2. Turn the work and continue back on a total of 50% of the stitches (32

sts of a 64-stitch sock). Place the remaining 25% of the stitches on a holder to work later for the heel.

3. Work back and forth on these stitches until the instep measures 2 inches less than the total foot length, measured from the split point at the end of the leg.

The Foot

Once the instep shaping is finished, the foot will then be worked on in a straight manner without any other shaping till the sock feet measures a length of 2"/5cm short of the preferred length from the heel's end to the toe's end. When the foot is being worked on, the color pattern or the original stitch that is established in the cuff is resumed. In some instances, nevertheless, stitches that are highly textured like some lace patterns or ribs are rid of the foot's sole in order to provide more comfort for the wearer.

Below is a ***guide for knitting the foot.***

Once the gusset decreases are complete or waste yarn knit in, you knit the body of the foot. For a plain stockinette stitch sock, simply knit every stitch of every round until the foot length measures 2 inches less than the desired total length (approximately at the base of the big toe for adult socks).

Foot sizing is extremely variable, particularly foot length. Luckily, handknit socks are extremely stretchy and can accommodate a variety of sizes.

US Size	Eur Size	Sock Size	Foot Circumference (in)	Foot Length (in)
C 7-8	23-24	Child's S	5.5	6
C 9-11	25-28	Child's M	6.5	7
W/M 1-3	30-34	Child's L	7	8
W 5-7	36-38	Women's S	7.5	8.5
W 7.5-8.5	39-42	Women's M	8	9.5
W 9-11	41-42	Women's L	8.5	10.25
M 7-8.5	40-42	Men's S	9	10.5
M 9-10	43-44	Men's M	9.5	11
M 11-12	45-46	Men's L	10	11.5

In a patterned sock, you carry the stitch pattern across the top of the foot but work the instep in stockinette stitch. You work the pattern stitch over the two needles holding the stitches of the top of the foot, while working stockinette over the other two needles.

The Toe

In case the stitches are not in the right alignment, they will be shifted in order for some stitches to be on the second needle and the other half of the stitches to be divided to the first and third needle. Later, double decreases will be worked at each of the side edges of the toe till the expected remaining stitches number is arrived at. The stitches of the toe will be together woven with the *Kitchener stitch* till the sock is finished.

Below is a step-by-step **guide for knitting a basic rounded toe**.

A sock toe is shaped with decreases, with the exception of the short-row toe. Each toe is about 2 inches long, so the leg is worked until 2 inches from the desired length, measured from the back of the heel. The toe is most often worked in stockinette stitch, even if the leg and foot are patterned.

In the Basic Round Toe, you work decreases on the sides of the sock to the tip of the toe, which is then closed.

The round begins at the middle of the bottom of the sock:

1. Work the toe decreases.

Round 1: Needle 1: Knit to last 3 stitches, knit 2 together, knit1.

Needle 2: Knit 1, slip slip knit, knit to end of needle.

Needle 3: Knit to last 3 stitches, knit 2 together, knit1.

Needle 4: Knit 1, slip slip knit, knit to end of needle.

2. Work Round 2.

Round 2: Knit around on all stitches.

3. Repeat rounds 1 and 2 until you decrease the total number of stitches to 50%.

Be sure to end with a Round 2.

4. Repeat Round 1 only until approximately 2 inches' worth of stitches remain.

Between 10 and 18 stitches will remain depending on gauge. Continue to close the toe using the Kitchener stitch.

For a wider toe, decrease fewer times and leave more stitches to graft. For a narrower toe, decrease more times and leave fewer stitches to graft.

5. Arrange the stitches on the needles so that all the stitches from the top of the foot are on one needle and all the stitches from the bottom of the foot are on another needle, with the working yarn attached at one edge.

To close the tip of the toe, you can graft the stitches together using the Kitchener stitch. This creates a seamless closure at the end of the sock.

6. Cut the working yarn.

KNITTING SOCKS FOR BEGINNERS

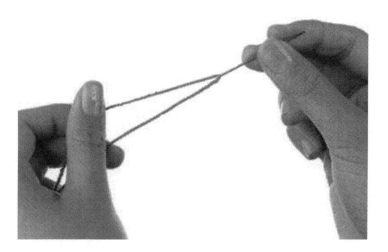

Leaving approximately 15 inches of yarn as a tail, thread the tail onto a darning needle.

7. Hold the sock with the needles parallel.

The working yarn should come off the back needle, on the right edge.

8. Bring the darning needle through the first stitch on the front needle purlwise.

9. Bring the needle through the first stitch on the back needle purlwise, and remove this stitch from the back needle.

10. Bring the needle through the next stitch on the back needle knitwise.

11. Bring the needle through the first stitch on the front needle knitwise, and remove this stitch from the front needle.

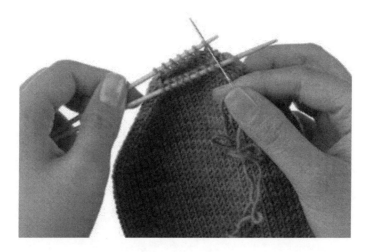

Repeat steps 4–7 until you work all the stitches.

12. Adjust the tension of the grafted stitches by carefully using the darning needle tip to pull up any slack in the stitches, working from right to left across the toe.

After you work most of the slack across to the left side of the toe, pull the tail of yarn to tighten.

13. Bring the tail to the inside of the sock and weave in the end.

So now that you've seen how to compose a sock, it's time to look at all of the stitches and techniques that will help you do this.

SOCK PATTERNS

This chapter will give you a few basic sock knitting patterns to practice. Now that you've learnt the stitches you'll need and you've seen the sock construct, you're ready to have a go at trying these. They will range from beginner to more advanced.

TOP/DOWN – A BASIC SOCK PATTERN

This is a basic top down sock pattern in fingering yarn and usually makes use of the basic toe and gusset heel. It entails specifications, sizing and well detailed data regarding how to work a heel of sock.

Difficulty Level:

Beginner

Size:

Children Medium

Required Materials:

Yarn: 200 yards of fingering weight

Needles: US Size 1 (2.¼mm) two circulars (double pointed), 1 longer circular needle.

Gauge:

8 stitches and 10 rounds = one 4 inch square.

Rib Stitch needed for Pattern:

Round 1: * Knit 1, purl 1 *, rep from * to * around.

Rep round 1 for pattern.

Basic top-down sock (make 2):

1. Cast on 52 stitches. Join, being careful not to twist.

2. Work ribbing (as above) until piece measures 1 inch from beginning.

3. Continue even in Stockinette stitch until piece measures 5.5 inches from beginning.

Work the heel

The heel is worked over 26 stitches.

1. Next row (Right Side): Knit 13 stitches, turn.

2. Purl across 26 stitches.

3. Row 1 (Right Side): * Knit 1, slip 1 *, repeat from * to * across.

4. Row 2 (Wrong Side): Slip 1, purl across.

5. Repeat rows 1 and 2 until you have worked 26 rows in total.

Turn the heel

1. Row 1: Knit across 15 stitches, slip slip knit, knit 1, turn.

2. Row 2: Slip 1, purl 5, purl 2 together, purl 1, turn.

3. Row 3: Slip 1, knit to 1 stitch before gap, slip slip knit (1 stitch from each side of gap), knit 1, turn.

4. Row 4: Slip 1, purl to 1 stitch before gap, purl 2 together (1 stitch from each side of gap), purl 1, turn.

5. Rep rows 3 and 4 until you have worked all heel stitches, ending if necessary on the last rep with knit 2 together and purl 2 together. 16 stitches remain.

Make the gusset

1. Next round: Knit Increase 8 stitches. Using an empty needle, knit 8 stitches. Rotate work and with the same needle, pick up 13 stitches along side of heel flap.

2. Work across 26 stitches of instep.

3. Pick up 13 stitches along other side of heel flap using an empty needle. Knit remaining 8 stitches. The heel is now complete and the round be-

gins at the center back heel.

Decrease for the gusset — Round 1

You will use a set of 4 needles for this.

1. Needle 1: Knit to last 3 stitches, knit 2 together, knit1.

2. Needle 2: Knit all stitches.

3. Needle 3: Knit all stitches.

4. Needle 4: Slip slip knit, knit 1, knit to end.

Decrease for the gusset — Round 2

1. Knit all stitches.

2. Repeat rounds 1 and 2 until 52 stitches remain.

3. Work even on these stitches until piece measures 5.5 inches from the back of the heel, or 2 inches less than desired total foot length.

Shape the toe

Round 1

1. Needle 1: Knit to last 3 stitches, knit 2 together, k1.
2. Needle 2: Slip slip knit, knit 1, knit to end.
3. Needle 3: Knit to last 3 stitches, knit 2 together, knit 1.
4. Needle 4: Slip slip knit, knit 1, knit to end.

Round 2

1. Knit all stitches.
2. Rep rounds 1 and 2 until 26 stitches remaining.
3. Rep round 1 until 12 stitches remaining.
4. Knit to the end of Needle 1. Cut yarn and graft toe.
5. Weave in ends and block.

ABSINTHE SOCKS

Difficulty Level:

Beginner

Size:

Women's Small

Required Materials:

Yarn: 2 skeins of merino superwash sports weight yarn.

Needles: Circular needles, size 1 (2.25mm).

Gauge

32 stitches and 48 rows = 4 inches in the stockinette stitch.

Pattern Notes

Toe

Cast on 16 stitches between 2 circular needles (8 stitches on each needle).

Round 1: Knit across.

Round 2: *Knit 1, Make 1, Knit to last stitch.

Next round, rearrange sts on needles to setup for heel:

Knit 1, purl 15 with Needle 2.

With Needle 1, purl 6, knit 20, purl 6.

With Needle 2, purl 15, knit 1.

You'll now have 32 stitches on Needle 1 and 56 stitches on Needle 2, and you'll be in position to work the heel.

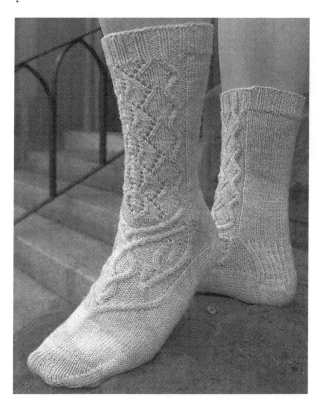

Heel

The heel will be worked back and forth only on the center 24 stitches of Needle 2, ignoring the gusset stitches for now).

Row 1, setup [Right Side]: Knit 23, wrap & turn.

Row 2 [Wrong Side]: Purl 22, wrap and turn.

Row 3 [Right Side]: Knit 21, wrap and turn.

Row 4 [Wrong Side]: Purl 20, wrap and turn.

Row 5 [Right Side]: Knit 19, wrap and turn.

Row 6 [Wrong Side]: Purl 18, wrap and turn.

Row 7 [Right Side]: Knit 17, wrap and turn.

Row 8 [Wrong Side]: Purl 16, wrap and turn.

Row 9 [Right Side]: Knit 15, wrap and turn.

Row 10 [Wrong Side]: Purl 14, wrap and turn.

Row 11 [Right Side]: Knit 13, wrap and turn.

Row 12 [Wrong Side]: Purl 12, wrap and turn.

Row 13 [Right Side]: Knit 11, wrap and turn.

Row 14 [Wrong Side]: Purl 10, wrap and turn

Turn the Heel

Next row (Right Side): *Knit 1, Slip 1* 5 times across unwrapped stitches, Knit each wrapped stitch together with its wrap, turn. Purl 17, Purl each wrapped stitch with its wrap, turn.

Right Side: *Slip 1, Knit 1* across 24 stitches, Slip 1, Knit last heel flap st together with first gusset stitch, turn.

Wrong Side: Slip 1, Purl 26, Purl last heel flap stitch together with first gusset stitch, turn.

Continue in this manner, working 1 gusset stitch together with the heel flap every row until all gusset stitches have been decreased. Decrease will end with a Wrong Side row.

Turn work and Knit across heel stitches. 56 stitches remain on both needles.

Leg

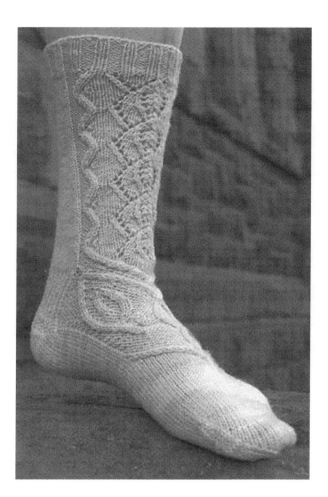

Transfer two stitches from both ends of Needle 2 to Needle 1. There will be 32 stitches on Needle 1 and 24 stitches on Needle 2.

First round of leg: Work the setup row of the leg chart on the stitches on Needle 1, and work the stitches on Needle 2 in stockinette stitch as established.

Continue working leg chart on Needle 1 and stockinette stitch on Needle 2, until 5 full repeats of chart have been worked - a total of 70 rounds.

Cuff

Ribbing round: *Knit 2, purl 2* to end of round.

Work 12 Ribbing rounds total.

Bind Off in rib pattern loosely.

Finishing

Weave in ends.

TUBE SOCKS

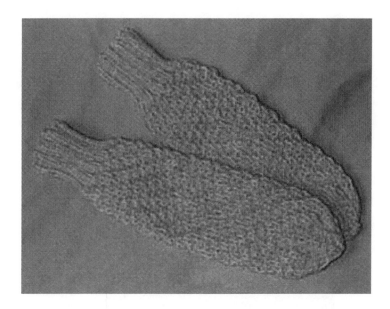

Due to the fact that it is not necessary to have the heel turned, tube socks are very easy to knit. This is a very easy pattern that can be enjoyed by even beginner knitters. These socks are **flatly knit on two needles and a side seam sewn**.

Among knitters, the most fashionable tube sock pattern is **knit using spiral ribbing**. This is made by a shift of the ribbing pattern after every few rows. This consequently causes the rib to have diagonal lines instead of the usual in place of the vertical lines. The stitch pattern comfortably holds the foot and is able to get back into shape easily. You can begin this by trying out the spiral tube socks for babies.

Tube socks are a magnificent gift idea as there's no need to know the exact length of the foot. You can just go ahead and knit a number of pairs in an adult's or child's size and rest assured that they will fit the recipient that you have chosen.

Difficulty Level:

Beginner

Size:

Children's Small

Required Materials:

Yarn: 2 skeins of Fingering weight yarn

Needles: Size No. 1 U.S. (2 ¼ mm) needles (double pointed)/ set of four

Size No. 3 U.S. (3. ¼ mm) needles (double pointed)/ set of four

Gauge

7 stitches = 1 inch in stockinette stitch.

Pattern Notes

Use smaller needles, Cast on 36 stitches.

Divide these stitches over three needles then join.

Knit 2, purl 2 and rib stitch for 2 inches.

Now, change to large needles and start the **spiral pattern**.

About Spiral Pattern

Round No. 1: Purl1, *Knit 2, Purl 2* now, repeat from * to *, ending Knit 2, Purl1

Round No. 2: Repeat Round 1

Round No. 3: *Purl 2, Knit 2* repeat from * to *

Round No. 4: Repeat Round 3

Round No. 5: Knit 1, *Purl 2, Knit 2* repeat from * to *, ending Purl 2, Knit 1

Round No. 6: Repeat Round 5

Round No. 7: *Knit 2, Purl 2* repeat from * to *

Round No. 8: Rep Round 7

Repeat these 8 rounds for 6½" (or desired length).

Shape Toe

Round No. 1: At beginning of each needle Knit 1, Slip 1, Knit 1 pass slipped stitch over, knit to last three sets of Knit 2 together, Knit 1

Round No. 2: Knit across.

Repeat these 2 rounds until 12 stitches remain. Knit 2 together around.

Cut yarn and thread through remaining sets. Pull to close and weave in end on Wrong Side.

TOE-UP SOCKS

One benefit of knitting socks beginning from the toe all the way to the top is that **the sock can be tried on and tested even as the knitting is in progress**. It's quite a new technique which allows you to make changes as you go – perfect for those new to knitting.

Difficulty Level:

Beginner

Size:

Children's Medium

Required Materials:

Yarn: 200 yards of fingering weight

Needles: US 1 (2.25mm) double pointed needles, two circulars, or one long circular needle

Gauge:

8 stitches and 10 rounds = 4 inches in stockinette stitch

Pattern Notes

- 2 x 2 ribbing

Round 1: * Knit 2, purl 2 *, repeat from * to * around.

Repeat round 1 for pattern.

- Flat stockinette stitch

Row 1: Knit.

Row 2: Purl.

Repeat rows 1 and 2 for pattern.

Start with the Easy Toe:

1. Provisionally cast on 10 stitches with waste yarn.
2. Work 4 rows in flat Stockinette stitch.

3. Rotate the work so that the provisional cast-on is at the top. Undo the provisional cast-on and place the live stitches evenly onto 2 empty double pointed needles. You are now ready to begin working in the round.

4. Round 1 (using a set of 4 needles):

Needle 1: Knit 1, make 1, knit 4. Take up an empty needle.

Needle 2: Knit 4, make 1, knit 1. Take up an empty needle.

Needle 3: Knit 1, make 1, knit 4. Take up an empty needle.

Needle 4: Knit 4, make 1, knit 1. Take up an empty needle.

Place a marker in the work to indicate beginning of round.

5. Round 2:

Needle 1: Knit 1, make 1, knit to end of needle.

Needle 2: Knit to last stitch, make 1, knit 1.

Needle 3: Knit 1, make 1, knit to end of needle.

Needle 4: Knit to last stitch, make 1, knit 1.

6. Round 3: Knit.

7. Repeat rounds 2 and 3 until you have 52 stitches in total.

Work the Foot

Now you start working the foot. Work even in stockinette stitch on these stitches until piece measures 5.5 inches from the tip of the toe, or 2 inches less than desired total foot length. Here you can incorporate different stitch patterns, such as ribbing, lace, or cables to add interest to the sock.

Turn the Heel

Work the heel over 26 stitches.

1. Row 1 (Right Side): Knit 25 stitches onto one needle. Wrap the

next stitch and turn.

2. Row 2 (Wrong Side): Purl 24 stitches. Wrap the next stitch and turn.

3. Row 3: Knit to 1 before previously wrapped stitch. Wrap the next stitch and turn.

4. Row 4: Purl to 1 before previously wrapped stitch. Wrap the next stitch and turn.

5. Rep rows 3 and 4 until 12 stitches remain unwrapped in the middle of the heel.

Pick up wraps

1. Row 1 (Right Side): Knit to wrapped stitch. Pick up wrap and work together with stitch. Wrap the next stitch and turn.

2. Row 2 (Wrong Side): Purl to wrapped stitch. Pick up wrap and work together with stitch. Wrap the next stitch and turn.

3. Row 3: Knit to double-wrapped stitch. Pick up both wraps and work together with stitch. Wrap the next stitch and turn.

4. Row 4: Purl to double-wrapped stitch. Pick up both wraps and work together with stitch. Wrap the next stitch and turn.

5. Repeat rows 3 and 4 until you have worked all wrapped stitches. On last pair of rows, pick up double wraps and work together with last heel stitch, then wrap the following stitch and turn.

6. Work 1 round even, picking up single wraps at sides of heel.

7. Work even on these 52 stitches until leg measures 4.5 inches from end of heel or desired length of leg minus 1 inch.

8. Work 1 inch of 2 x 2 ribbing. Bind off all stitches loosely.

9. Repeat all steps for second sock.

10. Weave in ends and block.

If there are any holes or gaps at the top of the heel, you can close them up by running a bit of yarn around the gap and tightening to close it up. Weave in the ends and block normally.

PLAIN SOCKS

This usual conventional sock is usually knit from top to bottom and is generally knit across the globe. This pair of socks consists of the top ribbing exercise, heel, leg, foot and then toe knit following in that order. This pattern has a textured pattern incorporated with the basic formula of the socks.

Difficulty Level:

Beginner

Size:

Children's Small

Required Materials:

Yarn: 2 skeins of 3 ply fingering weight yarn

Needles: 1 pair of No. 1 single pointed needles.

Stitch holder.

Gauge

8 ½ stitches = 1 inch

Pattern Notes

Starting at the cuff: Cast on 40 stitches

Work in ribbing of knit 1 then purl 1, for 1 ½ inches.

On the last row decrease to 36 stitches.

Now work in stockinette stitch until the piece measures 3 ½ inches in all.

Heel:

Knit 10 stitches.

Leave on the needle, then place the next 16 stitches for instep onto a stitch holder.

Place the remaining 10 stitches onto a 2nd stitch holder.

Working on the 10 stitches in stockinette stitch always slipping the first stitch on a purl row, to make 14 rows.

End with a purl row.

Turn the Heel:

Knit 2, slip 1, knit 1, pass slipped stitch over, knit 1, turn; slip 1, purl 3, turn.

Knit 3, slip 1, knit 1, pass slipped stitch over, knit 1, turn; slip 1, purl 4, turn.

Knit 4, slip 1, knit 1, pass slipped stitch over, knit 1, turn; slip 1, purl 5, turn.

Knit 5, slip 1, knit 1, pass slipped stitch over, knit 1.

With the same needle pick up and knit 8 stitches along side of heel.

Knit the 16 stitches off stitch holder onto needle; place these 30 stitches onto a free stitch holder.

Knit the 10 stitches from stitch holder.

Work on these stitches for 15 rows, (always slipping the first stitch on a knit row), ending with a knit row.

Shaping 2nd Half of Heel:

Purl 2, purl 2 together, purl 1, turn; slip 1, knit 3, turn.

Purl 3, purl 2 together, purl 1, turn; slip 1, knit 4, turn.

Purl 4, purl 2 together, purl 1, turn; slip 1, knit 5, turn.

Purl 5, purl 2 together, purl 1.

With the same needle, pick up end purl 8 stitches along side of heel.

Place a marker on the needle.

Purl 16 stitches of the instep, place a marker

Purl remaining 14 stitches.

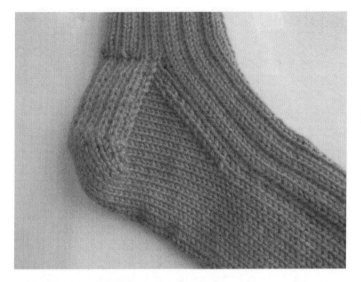

Decreases:

1st Decrease: Knit to within 3 stitches of first marker.

Knit 2 together, knit 1; place slip marker; knit 16 stitches: place slip marker; knit 1, slip 1, knit 1. Pass slipped stitch over, knit to end of row.

2nd row: Purl across row, keeping markers in place.

Repeat these last 2 rows until 36 stitches remain on the needle.

Drop off the markers.

Work even in stockinette stitch until the sock measures 4 inches from the back of heel, ending with a knit row.

Purl 9 stitches; place a marker on needle; purl 18 stitches; place a marker on needle; purl 9 stitches.

Toe Decreases:

Knit to within 3 stitches of first marker, knit 2 together, knit 1; place slip marker; knit 1, slip 1, knit 1, pass slipped stitch over, knit to within 3 stitches of 2nd marker; knit 2 together, knit 1; place slip marker, knit 1, slip 1, knit 1, pass slipped stitch over, knit to end of row.

2nd row: Purl across row, keeping markers in place.

Repeat these last 2 rows until 12 stitches remain in all, ending with a knit row.

Purl across next row; purling 2 stitches together across.

Break yarn leaving 10 inches. Thread a darning needle and draw through all stitches, fasten tight on the wrong side.

Sew sole and back seams.

Make the other sock the same way.

BLASTED TOE SOCKS

For that knitter who loves adventure, it is worth trying the blasted toe sock pattern. This sock type may not be a walk over exercise for the beginner but would come in handy for a more experienced and advanced knitter. This type of sock is very warm and also offers cozy cushioning for the feet balls.

Difficulty Level:

Intermediate.

Size:

Adult Small.

Required Materials:

Yarn: 100 yards of worsted weight yarn.

Needles: Size No. 3 double pointed needles.

Stitching marker

Safety pins or stitch holder

Tapestry Needle

The Gauge

20 stitches = 4 inches in Stockinette stitch

Pattern Notes

Cast on 34 stitches.

Divide these stitches among the 4 double pointed needles then join.

Now place marker and mark the start of round

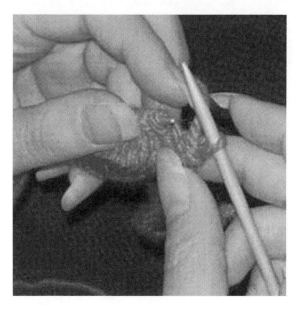

Rounds 1 – 10: *Knit through back loops, Purl 1* repeat this to stitch marker.

Rounds 11 – 40: Knit across.

Round 41A: Shape the toes. Knit 11 sets, cast on 3 more stitches, now place next 12 stitches on holder (for this, use safety pins), now knit remaining 11 stitches back to the start of round.

Now you should have around 25 stitches divided on the double pointed needles.

KNITTING SOCKS FOR BEGINNERS

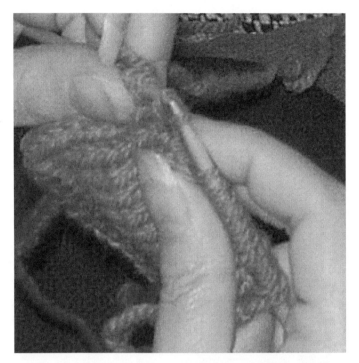

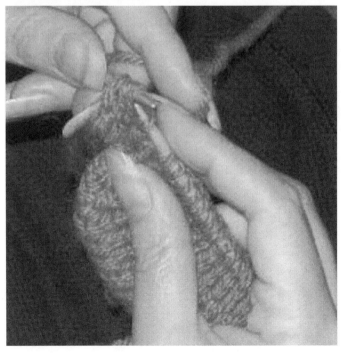

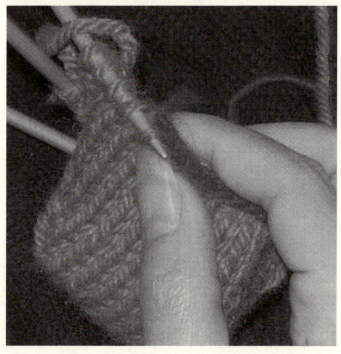

Rounds 42A – 45A: Knit around 25 stitches evenly.

Rounds 46A – 50A: Now Purl 1,*Knit through back loops, Purl 1* repeat to marker.

Now bind off those sets loosely.

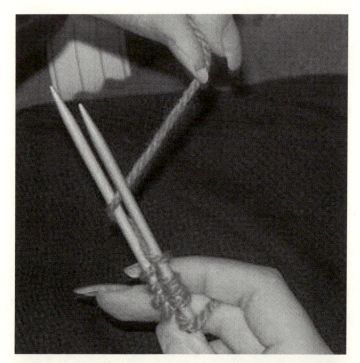
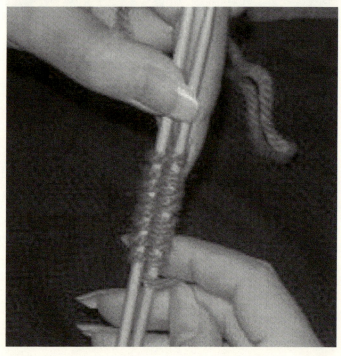

KNITTING SOCKS FOR BEGINNERS

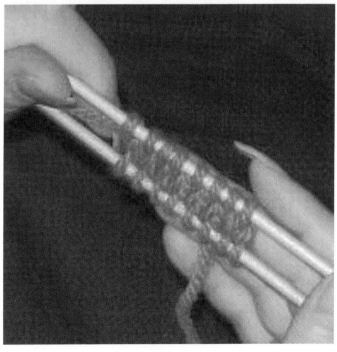

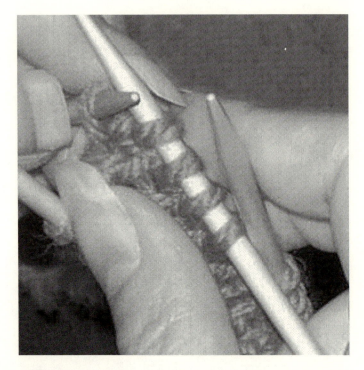

Round 41B: Shape the big toe. By knitting across those 12 stitches on the holders, and on 3 more stitches, which you cast on following to the 3 sets of 41. Now place marker.

Rounds 42B –45B: Knit 15 stitches evenly.

Round 46B: Now knit 2 together, purl 1, *Knit through back loops, purl 1* repeat from * to * to stitch marker.

Rounds 47B – 50B: Now *Knit through back loops, purl 1* repeat to marker.

Bind off these 14 stitches loosely.

KNITTING SOCKS FOR BEGINNERS

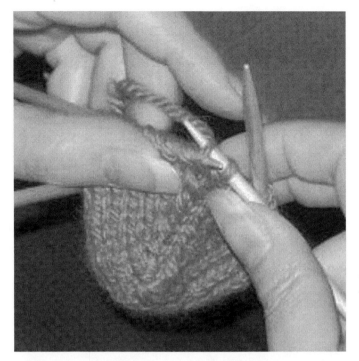

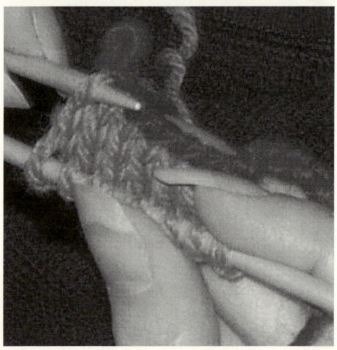

Now repeat all this for the second sock.

Finishing

Weave in the ends using the tapestry needle.

AIR RAID SOCKS

The Air Raid sock pattern is a pattern that is not only fun to knit but also an easy one to understand. It assumes a vertical geometrical design that reminds one of dropping bombs. This pattern is quite addictive and will tempt you to sit in your knitting chair all day long.

Initially known as *Seaweed socks*, the Alaria sock is an ideal sock pattern for yarns that are hand painted, color on color, variegated and handspun. This sock yarn is made of kelp material, which grows abundantly across the globe.

The kelp forests are an important environmental part that assists greatly in cleaning the oceans, feeding the aquatic life as well as humans and also confiscates carbon dioxide.

Difficulty Level:

Intermediate

Size:

Adult Medium

Materials Needed:

Yarn: 100 grams of variegated worsted weight yarn.

Needles: Size No. 1 double pointed needles.

Tapestry needle.

Gauge

9 stitches = 1 inch in stockinette stitch.

KNITTING SOCKS FOR BEGINNERS

Pattern Notes

Cast on 60.

Knit 1 through back loops, 1purl 1 around. Continue (raised ribbing) for 1/2 inch.

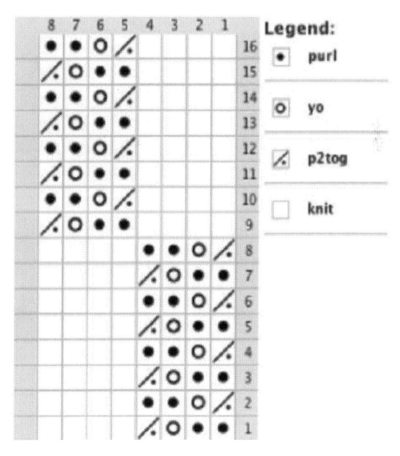

Rows 1 – 2 : Knit 4, purl 2. Repeat across.

Rows 3 – 4: Knit 3, purl 3. Repeat across.

Rows 5 – 6: Knit 2, purl 4. Repeat across.

Rows7– 8: Knit 1, *purl 4, knit 2* repeat from * to *, ending with knit 1.

Rows 9 – 10: Knit 1, *purl 3, knit 3* repeat from * to *, ending with knit 2.

Rows 11 – 12: Knit 1, *purl 2, knit 4* repeat from * to *, ending with knit 3.

Repeat until you get to the point where the sock leg reaches 7 or 8 inches in length (or as desired.)

Work the Heel

Heel Row 1: Knit 30. Now turn work.

Heel Row 2: Slip 1, Purl 1, and then repeat across.

Repeat these rows 15 times (or desired length).

Turn the Heel

Row No. 1: Slip 1, purl 17, purl 2 together, purl 1. Then turn work.

Row No. 2: Slip 1, knit 6, slip slip knit, knit 1. Then turn work.

Continue until every heel stitches complete.

The Gusset

Pick and knit around 15 stitches alongside of the heel flap.

Now knit across in the pattern as set.

Then pick and knit again 15 stitches.

Now knit 1 more row around. (Upon the instep stitches, continue the pattern)

Now knit 1 slip slip knit, then knit to remaining 3 stitches prior to instep, knit 2 together, knit 1.

Continue rows No. 1 and 2, now decrease every other row as well as work pattern on the instep till you reach down to around 30 stitches at the foot. This way, continue in the pattern till the foot is about two inches below the desired length.

Now decrease rounds: knit 1, slip slip knit, knit to three stitches lasting on the needle, knit 2 together, knit across. Repeat for the foot stitches.

After that, knit around.

This way, repeat 2 rounds till 8 stitches remaining on the instep needle, now 16 stitches together.

Grafting the Toe

Weave it in all the ends. Repeat for the second sock.

FAIR ISLE SOCKS

These magnificent Fair Isle socks are beautiful and just feel good on your feet. The pattern looks complex, and may be more challenging than the previous socks you've knitted during this book, but the end result looks amazing.

Difficulty Level:

Advanced

Size:

Women's Medium

Materials Needed:

Yarn: 4 skeins of worsted weight yarn in varying colors.

Needles: 4mm needles.

Gauge:

4 stitches = 1 inch.

Pattern Notes

Cuff:

Using 4mm needles and yarn A cast on 50 stitches

Row 1: * knit 2, purl 2* repeat from * to * until last 2 stitches, knit2

Row 2: * purl 2, knit 2* repeat from * to * until last 2 stitches, purl 2

These rows set 2x2 rib

Rows 3-26: work in 2x2 rib

Reindeer Pattern:

Change to stockinette stitch.

Rows 27-29: Include 1 stitch at each end of each row. 56 stitches

Row 30: Purl across.

Note: Letter following instruction in brackets = color to be used.

Row 31: * knit 6 (B), knit 1 (A), knit 7 (B)*, repeat from * to * across.

Row 32: * purl 6 (A), purl 1 (B), purl 1 (A), purl 1 (B), purl 5 (A)*, repeat from * to * across.

Row 33: * knit 3 (A), knit 1 (B), knit 1 (A), knit 1 (B), knit 1 (A), knit 1 (B), knit 1 (A), knit 1 (B), knit 4 (A)*, repeat from * to * across.

Row 34: * purl 4 (A), purl 1 (B), purl 1 (A), purl 1 (B), purl 1 (A), purl 1 (B), purl 1 (A), purl 1 (B), purl 3 (A)*, rep from * to * across.

Row 35: * knit 3 (A), knit 1 (B), knit 5 (A), knit 1 (B), knit 4 (A)*, repeat from * to * across.

Row 36: * purl 4 (A), purl 7 (B), purl 3 (A)*, repeat from * to * across.

Row 37: using yarn A knit to end.

Row 38: using yarn A purl to end.

Row 39: * knit 7 (A), knit 1 (B), knit 6 (A)*, repeat from * to * across.

Row 40: * purl 4 (A), purl 1 (B), purl 1 (A), purl 2 (B), purl 6 (A)*, rep from * to * across.

Row 41: * knit 8 (A), knit 2 (B), knit 4 (A)*, repeat from * to * across.

Row 42: * purl 2 (A), purl 3 (B), purl 9 (A)*, repeat from * to * across.

Row 43: * knit 4 (A), knit 1 (B), knit 4 (A), knit 2 (B), knit 3 (A)*, repeat from * to * across.

Row 44: * purl 3 (A), purl 6 (B), purl 5 (A)*, repeat from * to * across.

Row 45: * knit 5 (A), knit 6 (B), knit 3 (A)*, repeat from * to * across.

Row 46: as Row 44

Row 47: * knit 4 (A), knit 1 (B), knit 6 (A), knit 2 (B), knit 1 (A)*, repeat from * to * across.

Row 48: * purl 1 (A), purl 1 (B), purl 8 (A), purl 1 (B), purl 3 (A)*, repeat from * to * across.

Row 49: * knit 2 (A), knit 1 (B), knit 8 (A), knit 1 (B), knit 2 (A)*, repeat from * to * across.

Row 50-51: using yarn A continue in stockinette stitch

Row 52: using yarn B purl to end

Row 53: using yarn A knit to end

Rows 54-55: using yarn B continue in stockinette stitch.

Row 56-57: using yarn A continue in stockinette stitch.

Star Pattern:

Row 58: * purl 2 (C), purl 1 (D), purl 3 (C), purl 1 (B), purl 3 (C), purl 1 (D), purl 3 (C), repeat from * to * across.

Row 59: * knit 2 (C), knit 2 (D), knit 2 (C), knit 1 (B), knit 1 (C), knit 1 (B), knit 2 (C), knit 2 (D), knit 1 (C), repeat from * to * across.

Row 60: * purl 3 (D), purl 1 (C), purl 1 (B), purl 3 (C), purl 1 (B), purl 1 (C), purl 3 (D), purl 1 (C), repeat from * to * across.

Row 61: * knit 1 (C), knit 2 (D), knit 1 (C), knit 1 (B), knit 5 (C), knit 1 (B), knit 1 (C), knit 2 (D), repeat from * to * across.

Row 62: * purl 1 (D), purl 1 (C), purl 1 (B), purl 1 (C), purl 5 (B), purl 1 (C), purl 1 (B), purl 1 (C), purl 1 (D), purl 1 (C), repeat from * to * across.

Row 63: * knit 2 (A), knit 1 (B), knit 1 (A), knit 3 (B), knit 1 (A), knit 3 (B), knit 1 (A), knit 1 (B), knit 1 (A), repeat from * to * across.

Row 64: * purl 1 (B), purl 1 (A), purl 3 (B), purl 3 (A), purl 3 (B), purl 1 (A), purl 1 (B), purl 1 (A), repeat from * to * across.

Row 65: * knit 1 (B), knit 6 (A), knit 1 (B), knit 6 (A), repeat from * to * across.

Row 66: as Row 64

Row 67: as Row 63

Row 68: as Row 62

Row 69: as Row 61

Row 70: as Row 60

Row 71: as Row 59

Row 72: as Row 58

Cut yarns B, C and D and continue in yarn A only

(Turning the Heel) Rows 73-74: work in stockinette stitch.

Work ten rows in 2x2 rib

Work 48 rows in stockinette stitch *at the same time* decrease one stitch at each end of 19th, 9th and 45th row.

Next row: knit 2 together to end

Cut yarn then thread tail though remaining stitches, pull tightly and fasten off

Work second sock to match

To make up

Weave in ends. Sew up side seams.

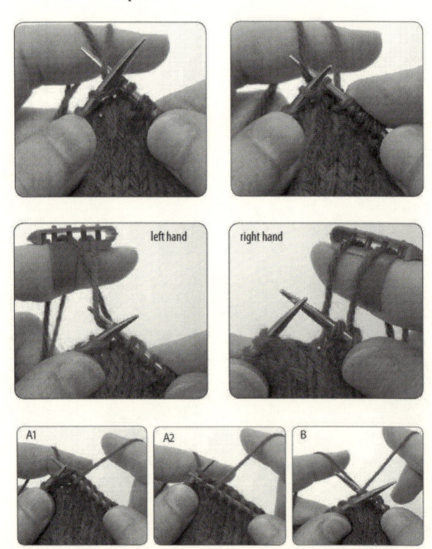

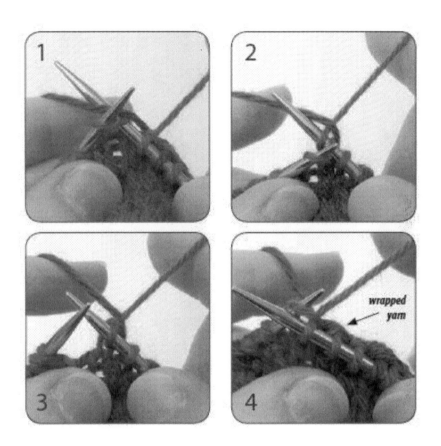

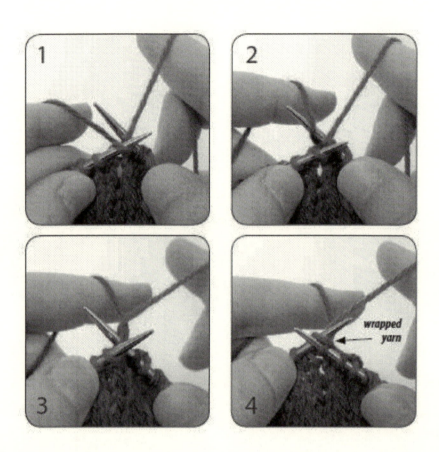

TIPS FOR LONG LASTING SOCKS

1. Avoid winding your yarn into a cake like piece till you get ready to knit. The winding may pull out the fibers and over time, the yarn is capable of losing its ability to get back into shape.

2. At all costs, the right yarn should be used for the project. 100% pure cotton may not be appropriate for socks since they will bag quickly and lose their shape when they are worn. Due to their intrinsic elasticity, the wool and nylon blends are quite popular.

3. Always select high quality sock yarn as cheap yarn will usually have short fibers that pill and wear out quite faster than the longer fibers. You may find good deals on sale in case you have a tight budget.

4. Always ensure that you choose one needle size or more as you knit the feet. In case a label demands for a US2 needles, you can knit the foot's sock on a US1 or US0 in order for you to obtain a dense fabric that can hold the wearer very well.

5. The correct size sock should be knit. Very big socks will usually slip around your foot and will cause more wear as they move round and round in your shoes.

6. Socks should be thoroughly rinsed before washing with other items. Even if dye is not expected to run, the colors that are quite saturated may run and you will not be happy when your other socks are affected.

7. When washing, always turn socks inside out. This way, the socks

inside will acquire a fuzzy halo with time on the inside and not on the outside.

8. Your finished socks need to be washed in a small mesh bag while in the machine so that they do not become snagged on zippers and hooks.

9. At no one time should you wash socks in hot water. This applies also to even those socks labeled as super wash, as they will shrink a bit or felt.

10. To dry the socks, lay them flat. Drying them by machine will lessen the stitch definition and make the socks look as if they have been worn for a long time. The fibers will be broken down from the intense drying heat.

TOP 5 TIPS FOR BEGINNERS

So now that you have experimented with a few knitting patterns, you may have stumbled across a few issues. With that in mind, this chapter covers a few tips to help you avoid, or at least overcome them.

Here are **Top 5 Tips for Beginners**:

1. *Start Big*

Starting with chunky yarn and big needles because then it will be easy to spot mistakes and unravel what you've done.

2. *Invest in Equipment*

Don't go nuts getting absolutely everything available because you will end up buying a lot of equipment you don't need. But, be sure to get:

- 2 pairs of needles
- Stitch markers
- A selection of basic, inexpensive yarn
- A sewing needle
- A bag or box to keep everything in

3. *Online*

There are many resources online which can help you get started. This book gives you all of the basics but there will come a point where you want more. Aside from YouTube which is filled with extremely useful videos from fellow knitters, the following websites are filled with useful information and other patterns to practice:

www.knittinghelp.com

www.knittingpatterncentral.com

www.lionbrand.com

4. Find a Friend

Having someone to knit with is always helpful. You can make the activity more sociable. If you don't know anyone who knits, there is a huge online community where people swap tips and discuss projects. A few of these forums include:

knittingforums.org.uk

knittinghelp.com/forum/

ravelry.com

5. Abbreviations

Keep a list of all the knitting abbreviations listed in this book handy for completing patterns. It's easy to forget what some of them might mean. If patterns include unusual or pattern specific abbreviations, they will list them. You can find all them in the chapter Knitting Glossary Terms below.

LEFT HANDED KNITTING

Don't be put off from knitting just because you are left-handed. It is very easily modified, as shown by the guide below.

Instead of casting on to the left-hand needle, you cast on to the right-hand.

The needle you work with is the left-hand needle while the right-hand needle holds the stitches you're working into.

Knitting and purling are the same concepts, where you still either work with the yarn behind your needle or in front of it. Your right side and wrong side of the fabric are still the same based on where those yarn bumps belong. A left-handed knitter just has to figure out how to make all of these basics feel natural without as much guidance as a right-handed knitter would find. Many left-handed knitters find that working in a mirror is great practice and helps them figure out the best ways to work.

TOP 3 COMMON KNITTING MISTAKES

Now we're going to look at some of the **most common mistakes in knitting and how to fix them.**

1. Stitches are too tight

One very common complaint that new knitters have is that their stitches are just getting too tight. There are a *few ways to overcome this*:

- Make sure you aren't knitting at the tips of your needles.
- Be sure to push the needle through the stitch correctly.
- Adjust the tension.

2. Fixing Incorrect Stitches

To fix a knit stitch make sure that the stitch from the previous round is on the left and the loose strand is on the right.

Then insert the right needle tip into the stitch from front to back, and pull the stitch over the loose strand and off the needle. The stitch is now complete.

To fix an incomplete purl stitch make sure that the stitch from the previous round is on the right and the loose strand is on the left. Insert the right needle tip through the stitch from back to front and slip the stitch to the right needle. Tip the right needle down slightly in front of the loose strand.

Push the loose strand through the stitch from front to back.

Place the stitch back onto the left needle and now it is ready for you to work.

Did you accidentally knit a stitch instead of purl it, or vice versa? Did you also not realize your mistake until you're on the next round? Fixing this mistake is a variation on picking up a dropped stitch.

Take the incorrect stitch off the left needle. Gently pull the strand of yarn running between the two needles. This pulls the stitch out by 1 round.

Pick up the stitch correctly. For a knit stitch, insert a crochet hook or the tip of a knitting needle into the stitch from front to back and pull the strand back through the loop to re-form the stitch.

For a purl stitch, place the loose strand in front of the stitch. Insert a crochet hook or tip of a knitting needle into the stitch from back to front.

Pull the strand through the loop from front to back. Place the corrected stitch back onto the left needle.

When working with some yarns, you can easily pick up only part of the yarn strand while knitting along. To correct a split stitch on the next round, take the stitch off the left needle and then replace it, taking care to place the needle through the entire stitch. To correct a split stitch several rounds down, ladder down and pick up the stitch in pattern, taking care to pull the entire strand through on each round when working back up to the needle.

3. Twisted Stitches

If your knitting stitches end up twisted, you will want to be able to fix them.

In a non-twisted stitch, the part of the stitch in front of the left needle appears to the right of the part of the stitch behind the needle. Sometimes, especially when picking up dropped stitches, the stitch ends up with the front leg to the left of the back leg, which creates a twisted stitch.

You can correct a twisted stitch in two ways.

Take the stitch off the left needle, turn it, and place it back onto the needle; it is now untwisted.

You can also correct a twisted knit stitch by knitting into the back of the stitch rather than the front. Insert the right needle tip into the stitch on the left needle through the back loop from right to left; the right needle is behind the left needle.

Wrap the yarn as for a knit stitch and pull the new stitch through from back to front. The stitch is now untwisted and correctly mounted for the next round.

When working in the round on double-points, two circular, or one long circular, sometimes *"gaps"* or *"ladders"* form at the junction of two needles. Pulling the needles in opposite directions creates tension on the stitches, which causes a gap.

The laddering effect is often more pronounced when using double-pointed needles because there are more junctions — four rather than the two you get when working with circulars.

To prevent ladders, pull the working yarn firmly on the first 2 stitches when switching needles. This helps to tighten the corners.

If you are still having trouble, try shifting the stitches from needle to needle as you knit around. This prevents a ladder effect because you disperse the loose stitches over the entire sock. However, some patterns assume that the stitches on each needle remain on the same needle for the course of the sock. Just make sure your stitches are on the right needles when knitting a heel or toe.

Knit to the last 2 stitches of the needle (double-pointed or circular).

Slip the last 2 stitches onto the next needle, taking care not to twist them, then knit across the next needle as usual to the last 2 stitches.

Repeat Step 2 as you go around to shift the stitches from needle to needle.

FAQ

1. What kind of yarn do I use for knitting socks?

Most knitters recommend a medium weight yarn for knitting socks as it's easier to work with and gives an extremely comfortable finish. Of course, as you experiment with varying patterns you'll develop your own preferences.

2. How do I knit a sock?

There are many different ways you can knit socks, as shown by the variation presented in this guide. There are many other free patterns that you can source online, such as the ones found at *knittingonthenet.com/socks.htm*.

3. How do you darn knitted socks?

- Thread your tapestry needle with up to about a yard of yarn. Starting several stitches away from the worn area, and at least two rows below it, work duplicate stitch over the knit fabric, leaving a yarn tail of at least 6 inches that will be later darned in.

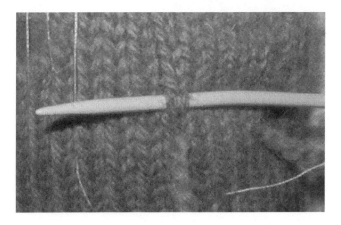

Needle inserted behind the top of the stitch you're starting with.

- To do this, pick a point to bring up the needle tip from inside to outside (illustrated in the picture above), at the base (bottom of the "V" shape a knit stitch makes) of a stitch. Then look carefully at the V shape of the stitch you're at the bottom of. Pass the point of the needle behind the V point just above that stitch, then out again. Pull the yarn through, being careful of how tightly you pull the yarn - you want the new yarn to sit snugly on the surface of the old, but not crumple the knit cloth.

- Now pass the point of the needle back into the fabric where it first came out, at the point of the bottom of this first stitch, and bring it out again at the point at the bottom of the next stitch over in the same row. Right handed people can do this most easily right to left, Left handed people probably will find it easiest to work left to right.

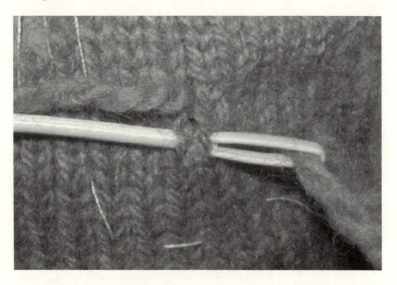

Needle inserted behind the bottom of the second stitch you're duplicating

- You've just 'duplicated' one knit stitch and started the next! As you keep moving through the row, you'll find you develop a rhythm and it goes much faster.

Watch your tension. You want your duplicated stitches to be nearly as possible the same size as the original stitches. They will lay on top of the knitting as it is, making bulkier area than you started with.

- At the end of the row, going several stitches past the worn area, turn so you're working upside down, still right to left for right handers, left to right for left handers.

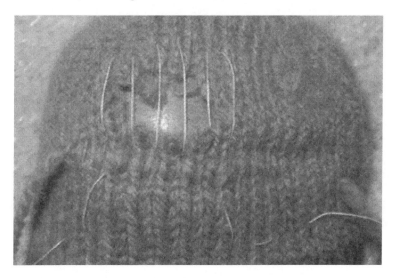

First row of duplicate stitch is completed below the hole

- The motion is a bit different since you're working upside down, but you now have the previous row to help guide your stitches. When your needle passes behind the V to come out again, make sure it goes into and out of the loops at the tops of the previous duplicate stitches. This will make more sense when you actually try it.

- Keep doing this back and forth. When you get to an actual gap in the stitches, you will understand the pattern that each stitch follows, and you will be able to 'fake' the stitches needed in that area. Tension is important. Don't pull too tightly, or too loosely, or the mended area will distort the cloth considerably.

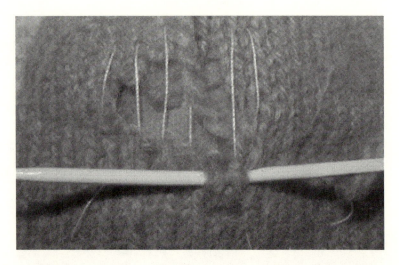

First row working into the hole, showing the needle going through the tops of two stitches from the row below.

- If you have a large hole and you have those vertical lines of sewing threads, you will see that your needle will pass behind a pair of threads to make the top portion of a stitch when there's not the V point of another stitch above it to go behind instead. I find this helps to keep the stitches I'm remaking from pulling out or getting messed up by the time I come back in the next row.

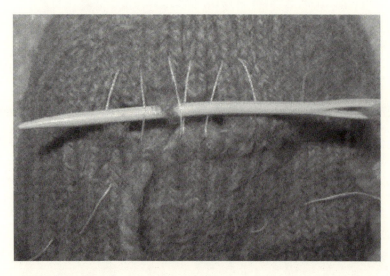

Here you see the needle passing behind the sewing thread framework to help shape a stitch in the middle of the hole

- When you have finished the row that reconnects with the knitting at the top of the hole, keep going at least two more rows. This will anchor the repair with 'healthy' stitches so it won't pull out when worn again.

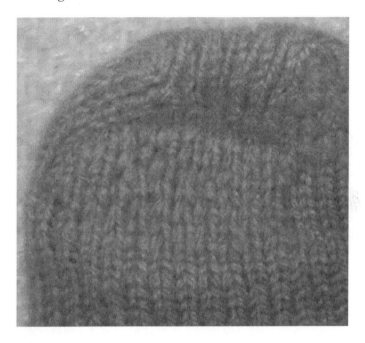

The darn is finished!

4. How to knit socks on 2 straight needles?

Many sock patterns – particularly those aimed at beginners – work from straight needles. You will have been able to practice a few of these whilst working through this book. If you're looking for more, a great resource is *audreyknits.webs.com/easytwoneedlesocks.htm*.

5. How do you knit socks on 4 needles?

You will have also seen patterns working on 4 double-pointed needles in this guide. If it's a technique you've enjoyed and you want to work more, try looking at *cometosilver.com/socks/SockClass_Start.htm*.

6. What's an easy pattern for knitting socks?

You have covered many patterns aimed specifically at knitting beginners for socks, but you can find a lot more at *allfreeknitting.com/Knit-Slippers-and-socks*.

7. How do you get high arches in knitting socks?

A sock with a heel flap and gusset is more accommodating for high arches.

8. Is it easier to knit socks with sock loom than using knitting needles?

Different people prefer different techniques for knitting. Now that you have gotten to grips with hand knitting using this book, it is likely that you'll prefer to work all of the necessary techniques by hand – but there is no harm in trying a loom! Many prefer the relaxation and methodical style of knitting that comes with doing it by hand – plus the level of satisfaction at a completed project.

9. Should you knit a swatch gauge?

It's always advisable, especially for beginners to knit a swatch gauge to make sure that you have chosen the correct yarn and needles for a pattern. Failing to do so can result in the finished project being the wrong size, and no one wants to waste time on that!

10. How to avoid the dreaded sock knitting gusset hole?

Here's a great guide to prevent this:

Step 1: A couple of rows before the start of the heel flap, place 3 stitches that correspond with the instep and 3 stitches that correspond with each side of the heel flap on a coil-less safety pin. This keeps the stitches on each side of the heel divide from stretching out as the heel flap is worked.

Step 2: Work the heel flap, heel turn, and gussets as normal. You can probably remove the safety pin after a few rows of gusset decreases, but I left it in for good measure.

Step 3: Remove the safety pins and marvel at how there is no hole to be found. Because the heel flap is worked in a contrasting color for these socks, there was a small hole on the other side where the new color was

joined. Once you weave it in, this disappears.

CONCLUSION

So, now that you have mastered all of the stitches needed to knit socks and practiced with the patterns included within this guide you have seen how easy a skill of knitting can really be! Now that you have been given the basics, you are able to go on to not only try out other knitting patterns, but also go on to create your own designs and try other projects too.

Sock knitting is one of the more challenging knitting skills, so now that you've gotten to grips with it, you have the basic skills needed to go on to try other garments, toys or home wares. Now that you have an invested interest in the hobby, why not meet other knitters and get involved with the community? Not only will you probably have local knitting groups in your area, there are a lot of online forums you can get involved with, such as:

www.ravelry.com

www.knittinghelp.com/forum

www.knittingparadise.com

Not only will these help you develop your skill further, you'll also make friends along the way! Knitting can be a great social activity as well as one that is great for your health.

Happy knitting!

KNITTING GLOSSARY TERMS

All knitters use a language that they understand best.

The following are the **commonly used abbreviations**:

* *:Repeat the instructions between the two asterisks

[ ]:work instructions in brackets as many times as directed

( ): work instructions in parenthesis as directed (also used to indicate size changes)

Alt: It means alternate (Like the "alt rows")

Beg: It means begin/beginning

Bet: It means between

BO: It means bind off

CA: It means color A (This is the case where there is above one color is being used)

CB: It means color B (Just as above)

CC: It means contrasting color

Cm: Centimeters

Cn: It means cable needle

CO: Cast On

Cont.: It means continue

Dec: It means decrease

DK: It means double knitting (a yarn weight or knitting technique)

Dp, dpn: It means double/pointed needle

EON: It means end of needle

EOR: It means end of row

FL: It means front loop

Foll: It means follow or following

G: It means Gram

G st: It means garter stitch (knitting every row)

Inc: It means increase

Incl: It means including

K: It means knit

K1 f&b: It means knit into the front of the stitch and later on to the back of the similar stitch

K tbl: It means knitting through the back loop, which establishes a twist on the completed stitch

K2 tog tbl: It means knit two stitches together

K2tog: It means knit two stitches together through the back loop instead of the front

Kwise: Knitwise

LC: It means left cross, a cable stitch where the front of the cross slants to the left

LH: It means left hand

Lp: It means loop

LT: It means left twist, a stitch that creates a mock cable slanted to the left

M: Meters

M1: It means make 1 stitch, which requires an increase method

M1 p-st: Make one purl stitch

MC: It means main color

Mm: Millimeters

Oz: Ounce

P: It means purl

P tbl: It means purl through the back loop instead of the front

P up: It means pick up

P2tog: It means purl two stitches together

P2tog tbl: It means purl two stitches together through the back loop instead of the front

Patt: It means pattern

Pm: It means place stitch marker

Prev: It means previous

Psso: It means mean pass slipped stitch over (as in binding off)

Pu: It means pick up (stitches)

Pwise: It means purlwise

RC: It means right cross, a cable stitch where the front of the cross slants to the right

Rem: It means remaining

Rep: It means repeat

Rev St st: It means reverse Stockinette stitch

RH: It means right hand

Rnd: It means round(s); when knitting on a circular or double pointed needle when it means the yarn is joined, you knit in rounds, not rows

RS: It means right side

RT: It means right twist, a stitch that creates a mock cable slanted to the right

Sk: It means skip

Sk2p: It means slip 1 stitch, knit 2 together, and then pass the slipped stitch over the knitted ones to create a double decrease

Skp: It means slip 1 stitch, knit 1 stitch, and then pass the slipped stitch over the knitted one to create a single decrease

Sl, slst, slip: It means slip or slide a stitch without working it

Sl, k1, psso: It means same as "skp"

Sl1k: It means slip 1 stitch knit-wise

Sl1p: It means slip 1 stitch purl-wise

sl st: It means slip stitch

Ssk: It means slip 1 stitch, slip the next stitch, and then knit the 2 stitches together to create a left/slanting decrease

Ssp: It means slip 1 stitch, slip the next stitch, and then purl the 2 stitches together to create a right/slanting decrease

Sssk: It means slip 1 stitch, slip the next stitch, slip the 3rd and then knit the 3 stitches together to create a double, left/slanting decrease

St: It means stitch

Sts: It means stitches

St st: It means Stockinette stitch; alternately knit a row and purl a row

Tbl: It means through the back loop (of a stitch)

Tog: It means together

WS: It means wrong side

Wyib: It means with yarn in back

Wyif: It means with yarn in front

Yds: Yards

Yfwd: It means yarn forward (same as yarn over)

Yo: It means yarn over, move yarn to the opposite direction

Yrn: It means yarn 'round' needle (same as yarn over)

yon: It means yarn over needle

ABOUT THE AUTHOR

Knitting has always been considered an old woman's game. But that was not the case with Emma Brown. As soon as she could hold a needle, her mother was trying to teach her how to knit. Though it took her a couple of years, until she could really maneuver those needles, once she had it down, she was a knitting machine.

Throughout her childhood, she was sitting beside her mother, and they would knit, day in and day out. For Christmas, all of her brothers and sisters received handmade socks and her friends all received colorful hats. For the first few years, they were lumpy and a little messy, but by age ten, she was a wizard with the yarn and the needles. Because socks were her favorite thing to make, and she could whip up a pair in only a few days, her family never lacked warm, comfortable socks.

In her teenage years, Emma discovered that many of her friends wanted to learn to knit. She gathered them up around her kitchen table, with needles in hand, and tried to teach them how to knit, just as her mother had taught her, all those years ago. They had all arrived with a different project in mind, and they all looked to her for guidance. As they stumbled over their first stitches, it was then when she first realized that there must be a better way. With everyone struggling to make a different project, she knew it would be nearly impossible to teach them all effectively.

That is when she first came up with the idea to find a better way to teach knitting. She had been told by several people that knitting seemed so difficult, that it was something you could learn if you had hours and hours a week to spend learning it. But she knew that it couldn't actually be that difficult. Millions of people already knew how to do it–it couldn't be that hard to teach!

Instead of again trying to teach her friends the way her mother had taught her, she began devising a new method. As she sat and thought, she knitted a pair of socks. As she knitted, she realized that socks were the perfect tool for teaching knitting. They included all of the basic techniques, and what you learned from sock knitting, you could easily use to follow just about any knitting pattern. She began writing down everything that could be learned from knitting socks, and then gathered her friends together again. With needles in hand, she explained the basic steps, and within three days, every last one of her friends had a brand new pair of socks, knitted by hand.

Now, you can tap into the same knowledge, draw on Emma's years of sock knitting experience, and learn to knit a pair of socks (and anything else!) in just three days!

Made in the USA
Middletown, DE
15 January 2021